MW00987742

Dear Reader,

Thank you for purchasing this book. We are excited that you have chosen to join us on the journey towards providing your pet dogs with healthy and nutritious meals.

We wanted to let you know that due to the high costs of print, we were unable to include any images in this book. Our goal was to make this book affordable for everyone, and we hope that the information provided is valuable to you even without visuals.

We appreciate your support, and we encourage you to reach out to us if you have any questions or feedback. Additionally, we invite you to consider leaving a review. We are dedicated to providing the best possible resources for dog owners, and we look forward to hearing from you.

Once again, thank you for choosing our book. We hope that it helps you provide the best possible care for your furry companion. Below you can find the link to our website which contains useful links to our social media pages, email addresses, and link to our Amazon page.

TABLE OF CONTENTS

ABOUT THE AUTHOR

I am happy to own a dog. When I was a little child, I developed a love for dogs, and it has only gotten stronger with time. I've had the good fortune to have several furry best friends in my life, each of whom is unique in their way. I wrote this book and shared my knowledge and experience with other dog owners because I am passionate about dogs.

I have spent years learning about and experimenting with homemade dog food recipes because I am a self-taught cook and dog lover. My mission is to help other dog owners in feeding their four-legged companions wholesome, delectable, and easily available prepared meals that are not only healthy for them but also beneficial for them. I am glad to share my recipes and knowledge with those who share my conviction that every dog deserves to have a healthy and happy life.

I enjoy spending time outdoors with my furry best friend when I'm not cooking for my dogs or writing about dog food. Nothing beats a long hike in the mountains or a stroll around the park with my dog by my side.

This book should motivate you to start preparing meals for your dog so it can get the nutritious food they need. I appreciate you choosing **"Homemade Healthy Dog Food Cookbook: The Only Simple Guide You Need to Learn to Make All Kinds of Healthy Dog Food – Including the Raw Dog Food Diet and Recipes for Healthy Dogs Treats & Desserts,"** and I hope you like it as much as I did while I was writing it.

INTRODUCTION

I've always been passionate about feeding my canine companion the healthiest diet possible. I still recall the day I brought home my first furry friend; a tiny Beagle named Max. I was very happy to welcome him into my family, but soon I concluded that I couldn't just feed him food from the shop. I needed to be certain that he was receiving the right nutrients for growth, therefore I wanted to know exactly what was going into his body. My quest to learn about and test out homemade dog food recipes was sparked by this.

I've observed the benefits it has had on my dogs' health and well-being over the years, which has taught me how crucial it is to give them balanced, nutritional meals. I decided to publish this cookbook to impart my wisdom and expertise to other dog owners. "Homemade Healthy Dog Food Cookbook" is a comprehensive manual for preparing wholesome, delectable, and inexpensive meals for your four-legged best friend.

The book is sectioned into two main sections, the first of which focuses on the theoretical side of making dog food from scratch. You will discover the advantages of making your own dog food in this section, along with tips on selecting healthy ingredients and making sure your dog eats balanced, nutritious meals. In order to give you peace of mind that your dog's meals are not only delectable but also secure for consumption, I have also included a section on food safety.

The book's second section, which concentrates on the recipes, is where the real fun starts. You can find a variety of recipes here that satisfy various dietary requirements and preferences, such as low-fat, grain-free, and gluten-free options. You can choose a recipe that your dog will enjoy, whether they favor meat or vegetables. You may easily make the dishes at home because each recipe comes with thorough instructions. You can be sure you're giving your dog wholesome, scrumptious meals without breaking the bank because the recipes use inexpensive, readily available ingredients.

This cookbook provides a variety of recipes that may be modified to meet different nutritional needs, such as bread and butter recipes, quick and simple recipes, vegan recipes, keto recipes, etc. Every recipe is prepared with healthy ingredients that are reasonable, accessible, and easy to find, enabling anybody to prepare healthy meals for their dog. This book is intended to assist you in giving your dog the finest nutrition available, regardless of your level of cooking experience.

The absence of finished dish photos in this book is one of its distinctive features. This is because including colorful graphics would greatly raise the cost of printing the book, and I want to make sure that everyone can buy it. In order to make it easy for you to make the recipes at home, I have instead concentrated on offering clear and straightforward directions.

This is the definitive manual for dog owners who want to feed their four-legged best friend healthy foods. This book will help you improve your dog's nutrition thanks to its simple directions, thorough discussion of the theory aspect, and variety of delectable homemade recipes.

Let's start cooking now! Rest assured that you are giving your four-legged best friend the healthiest, tastiest meals they have ever had thanks to the "Homemade Healthy Dog Food Cookbook."

CHAPTER ONE

NUTRITIONAL REQUIREMENTS

"What should I feed my dog?" is presumably the question that pet owners ask their veterinarians most frequently. To ensure your dog's overall health and well-being, be sure to feed them the right amount of nutritious food. You must understand the nutritional needs of dogs and how these needs have changed as a result of biological evolution in order to know how and what to feed your dog.

Dogs are carnivores; doesn't this mean they necessitate a diet high in animal products? The biological order Carnivora, which includes a sizable group of mammals with comparable tooth structures, includes species like dogs. Many animals in this order have different needs for food. Obligate or genuine carnivores are those members of this category who must consume meat in their diets at all times, although herbivores and omnivores can eat enough plant material to suit their nutritional needs. Cat is an example of an obligate carnivore, a cow is an example of an herbivore, and two examples of omnivores are dogs and humans.

Dogs' tooth structure and intestinal system have evolved to accommodate an omnivorous diet due to their nutritional requirements. This means that dogs can typically eat a variety of plant and animal foods to suit their nutritional demands. The quality and digestibility of these vital diet staples for dogs are more important than where the proteins and fats come from. Dogs can thrive if given a properly balanced vegetarian diet. An all-meat diet, however, would be imbalanced and fall short of meeting all of a dog's nutritional needs.

As the understanding of canine nutrition has grown as a result of basic and applied nutrition research, it is now understood that a well-balanced meal should also contain a sufficient amount of minerals, vitamins, certain important amino acids (from proteins), and some essential fatty acids (from fats). Depending upon a dog's stage of life (puppy, adolescent, adult, pregnant, and senior), different levels of these substances are required to carry out biological processes and create and maintain tissue.

WHAT INGREDIENTS SHOULD DOG FOOD HAVE?

Giving your dog the best food, you can afford is the best piece of feeding advice you can receive. Luxury food and inexpensive food differ in quality and origin but not in their nutritional content. Even though two dog foods may each contain 27% protein, their levels of digestibility may vary.

The ingredients of pet food are presented in weight order. An ingredient is weighed before being added to the food batch. For instance, fresh meat has a lot of water, however, a lot of it is lost during processing. Hence, it is possible that a dry diet high in corn would be more nutrient-dense than one high in meat.

The fact that some nutrients are stated as having a "minimum" percentage and others as having a "maximum" percentage adds to the difficulty because the actual batch of food may include a larger or lower percentage of the ingredient than is shown on the label.

Asking your veterinarian for advice on dog food selection is the best course of action. However, the following general advice can help you choose what to put in your dog's food bowl:

- Choose diets that contain identifiable, real, wholefood food ingredients. Find another diet if you aren't familiar with the majority of the stated ingredients.
- Choose a diet low in calories. The majority of adult, indoor, neutered, or spayed dogs require little energy. A cup of food for your dog should only have a few calories in it; ideally, no more than 350. If your dog weighs 20 pounds and your dog food has 500 calories per cup, the recommended serving size is low (and unappealing!). Even a few more kibbles from high-calorie foods can significantly increase weight-gain, making the situation worse.

DOG DIETS

There are numerous varieties of dog diets available, each with specific advantages and disadvantages. When selecting the ideal diet for your dog, it is crucial to take into account their individual requirements and medical concerns. The following are a few of the most popular dog diets:

Commercial dog food

For pet owners, commercial dog food is a very practical and accessible solution. These meals can be found in kibble, canned food, and even raw diets, among other forms. For dogs of all ages and breeds, commercial dog food is often enriched in vitamins, minerals, and other necessary ingredients. Commercial dog food, however, may also include fillers and artificial preservatives that are harmful to the health of your pet.

Homemade dog food
Dog food that is created from scratch with fresh ingredients that you buy from the grocery store is known as homemade food. You can modify this type of diet to match your dog's unique nutritional needs, and you have control over the standard of the contents. Additionally, homemade dog food is often less expensive than store-bought dog food. However, it may not contain all of the vitamins and minerals that your dog needs, and can take a while to prepare and store.

Grain-free dog food
Dog food that doesn't contain any grains or gluten is known as grain-free food. Dogs who could be sensitive to or intolerant to grains should be given this type of food. This type of food is also good for dogs with digestive problems because it may be easier for them to digest. It can cost more than other dog diets and it may not contain all the essential vitamins and minerals that your dog needs.

Low-fat dog food
Low-fat dog food is a sort of diet that is created for dogs who are obese or have other health issues that call for a low-fat diet. When compared to other dog diets, low-fat dog food often has less fat, which can aid in your dog's maintenance of a healthy weight. But it's crucial to pick low-fat dog food for your pet that still offers a healthy and balanced diet.

Vegetarian dog food
This type of diet excludes all animal products. Dogs that are sensitive to animal proteins, vegetarian/vegan food is a blessing. If this food is prepared using the necessary nutrients and vitamins, it can offer dogs a complete diet. However, finding high-quality vegetarian dog food can be very challenging, and not all dogs may benefit from it.

Dog diets come in a wide variety, and it's crucial to pick the right one for your pet based on their particular requirements and state of health. Whatever dog diets you decide to feed your dog, check with your veterinarian to ensure that your dog is receiving all the nutrients needed to maintain good health. You can improve and maintain your dog's general health and wellbeing for many years with appropriate nutrition and suitable diet plan.

WHAT SHOULD NOT BE OFFERED TO DOGS?

When it comes to grabbing tasty treats, dogs can be opportunistic, but not all common foods and drinks are suitable for them to consume. The following nine things should not be offered to dogs:

Onion, chives, and garlic

Whether dried, raw, or cooked, members of the onion family are particularly poisonous to dogs and can lead to digestive upset and red blood cell degeneration. Sometimes illness symptoms are not immediately noticeable and may take several days to manifest.

Chocolate

Despite the fact that both humans and dogs find chocolate to be tasty, it is another food that is deadly to dogs. Theobromine, a stimulant found in chocolate, is poisonous to dogs and can cause kidney failure.

Macadamia nuts

A macadamia nut toxin can harm your dog's muscles and nerve system, resulting in weakness, swollen limbs, and panting.

Corn on the cob

Your dog could perhaps die if it eats corn on the cob. Corn can be digested by dogs, but the cob can clog your dog's intestines.

Avocado

Avocados are yet another food that is bad for dogs. Avocado plants contain a substance known as persin in their leaves, fruit, and seeds that can cause dogs to vomit and suffer from diarrhea.

Artificial sweetener (Xylitol)
One must read the label before using a product as a treat for one's dog since the artificial sweetener Xylitol, which is often used in low-fat diet, and sugar-free meals and beverages, as well as some peanut butter, causes the release of insulin in bodies. However, if your dog ingests one of these sweetened treats, it could develop hypoglycemia, which is linked to liver failure and issues with blood coagulation.

Alcohol
Alcohol affects dogs significantly even with little consumption. Along with drunkenness, the beverage can also cause diarrhea, nausea, and perhaps injury to the central nervous system.

Cooked bones
Feeding your dog a raw bone to chew on is great, but avoid cooked bones at all costs. They quickly splinter when there are a lot of them, which can cause constipation or, in the worst instance, a catastrophic gut perforation.

Raisins and grapes
It's not just the fruit-form of raisins that should worry us as they are also found in many of the items we enjoy eating, like cakes, biscuits, and cereal. Although the toxin's actual active element is unknown, both grapes and raisins have the potential to seriously harm the liver and kidneys of a dog.

HOW MANY CALORIES SHOULD DOG FOOD HAVE?
The best way to know how many calories to feed your dog is to calculate its optimal lean weight and consider it while feeding the dog. This requires a continuous observation weighing for calories which may not always be feasible.

Depending on its lifestyle and body condition score, your veterinarian can determine how many calories your dog requires each day. You can use the below equation to determine the energy needs of an adult dog who stays inside your home, gets some light activity each day, and has been spayed or neutered:

Daily calorie needs = 30 x weight in kg (or pounds divided by 2.2) + 70

It is to know that this method is only a starting point because very few of our dogs are "average." The majority of dogs need fewer calories per day, while a few need a little bit more. This total daily calorie intake for your dog includes all meals, snacks, and treats. Your veterinarian may advise calorie restriction (which is often 70% to 90% of the calculated amount for weight maintenance) if your dog needs to reduce weight.

HOW OFTEN SHOULD A PET DOG BE FED?

Dogs' specific digestive and gastrointestinal characteristics from their biological evolution, as hunters, allow them to consume a substantial meal followed up to days without eating. However, it is advised to feed most pet dogs once or twice daily while two to three meals each day, evenly distributed, are beneficial for many dogs.

No matter what feeding schedule you decide on, don't let your dog go for a vigorous walk right after a big meal. Particularly when they finish their food quickly if they go for vigorous walk right away it may put them in the risk of getting abdominal issues i.e., bloating, intestinal blockage, or other severe digestive illnesses. Additionally, make sure that your dog has access to clean and fresh water.

CANNED OR DRY FOOD?

There are simply no difference between dry and canned (wet) dog food in terms of nutrients and digestibility. Your choice should be based on your lifestyle, tastes, and financial situation. Canned food could be a better option for dogs who need to drink more water or who have specific dietary requirements.

Otherwise, dry kibble will usually be sufficient for dogs.

Some dental meals made of dry kibble are properly prepared and can aid in mechanically removing plaque.

BREED VARIATIONS IN NUTRITIONAL NEEDS

Nutritionists and veterinary experts have discovered over the past few decades that there are different breed variations in metabolism and dietary requirements. Dog breeds that originated in particular regions, including those from the Arctic Circle and other aquatic breeds, may have adapted to specialized diets that are typical there. Due to inbreeding and genetic differences between individuals within each species, it becomes important to tailor a pet's diet to their individual needs to improve health.

You should take into account your dog's lifestyle in addition to its breed. Working dogs (such as those used for hunting, field trials, and herding) need different ratios of proteins and fats in their meals than sedentary house dogs or lap dogs.

The next chapter talks about tips for planning and preparing homemade dog food, including information on portion sizes, storage and food safety.

CHAPTER TWO

PLANNING, PREPARATION, AND STORAGE

Many dog lovers are switching from store-bought food to home-cooked meals for their pets as a result of the rising number of pet food recalls. It may become overwhelming if you've never done this before. You could know what to cook for your family and yourself, but you might not know what and how to prepare dog food.

As dog owners, we are often told not to share our food with our pets. What, then, do we cook? In reality, most human ingredients are OK. The difference is that the food we cook for ourselves often contains ingredients that are toxic to dogs or are too fatty or rich for their digestive processes. It is good to separately prepare food for them using healthy ingredients.

EFFECTIVE FEEDING PLAN FOR DOGS

It is quite easy to switch a dog to a natural diet plan, so please dismiss any worries you may have about raw feeding being difficult, unsafe, expensive, or time-consuming:

- To be successful, you only need to be aware of which ingredients are appropriate for your dog and in roughly what proportions.

- If you plan beforehand, it won't take you any longer than opening a can.
- Dogs are physically predisposed to consume raw food, and doing so is completely safe (Keep in mind that their stomach acids are strong enough to burn your fingers).
- Prime steak is not necessary for your dog! As indicated below, a dog will thrive on a variety of inexpensive ingredients.

There is no reason not to make a direct switch unless your dog has specific health difficulties (see chapter 5). In addition, it is not a bad idea to keep your dog fasting for a day prior to the switch if you can handle the looks of reproach. This will assist your dog in getting rid of the toxins that have accumulated due to a diet high in processed food.

An easy three-step process
Our simple adult dog feeding regimen is based on three basic (all-raw) ingredients and is the result of decades of experiments:
- Bone
- Meat
- Vegetable

The actual plan may be broken down into three easy steps:
- Take any minced or diced meat (chicken, cattle, lamb, hog, whatever)
- Add grated veggies (anything except raw potatoes) unless it is around two-third meat and one-third vegetables (in case you have a food processor, you can process the veggie in it).
- Purchase some meaty bones from the butcher and offer one to your dog every one to two days.

Follow the guidelines outlined later in this chapter for portion sizes. Use a variety of meat and vegetables.

APPROPRIATE INGREDIENTS

A list of all the different foods you can give your dog is provided below. An asterisk (*) indicates something important for your dog's wellness. The main purpose of the other ingredients is the additional nutrients that they offer.

- **Lean meat:** Chicken, beef, lamb, venison, rabbit, turkey, pork, and so on. It can be diced or minced.
- **Internal organs*:** Tripe, liver, the heart, and so on. The liver should never be more than 10% of the total diet. Where rape has been fed to an animal, beef liver must be avoided.
- **Fish:** Any type of fish, but especially fatty fish like sardines, herring, salmon, and pilchards. If you can't obtain fresh fish, you might wish to add a can of herrings or pilchards to the diet once or twice a week.
- **Dairy products:** Goat's milk, cheese, probiotic yogurt, and/or a little cottage cheese.
- **Eggs:** Any sort of whole egg is a great source of protein, vitamins, and omega fatty acids when consumed two or three times per week.
- **Bones*:** Preferably raw and meaty bones, especially from the carcasses of chicken or turkey.
- **Leafy vegetables*:** Broccoli, cauliflower, spinach, winter greens, etc.
- **Root vegetables*:** Carrots, parsnips, swede, turnips, etc. raw potatoes are not recommended because they are heavy in starch.
- **Fresh fruit:** Avoid grapes and avocados, and use dried fruit sparingly because of their high sugar content.
- **Extra oil*:** You may want to add some safflower, cod liver, hemp, flax seed, or sunflower oil once or twice a week.
- **Vegetable extracts:** Kelp, brewer's yeast, and/or a small amount of molasses.

You'll see that we don't specify how much, say, cod liver oil should be added. Make your own decisions. A teaspoonful will be sufficient for a small dog; however, you might want to add a tablespoonful for a very large dog.

SOME USEFUL TIPS

- Serving your dog meat, offal, and vegetables in their dish and providing them with raw and meaty bones on the side is the easiest method to meet their nutritional needs.
- When it comes to the ratio of meat, offal, and vegetables, there is no magic number. It is suggested mixing 1/3 vegetable with 2/3 meat and offal. Some may argue that 90% meat and offal and only 10% vegetables are preferable. So, consider each dog as an individual, and consider their preferences.
- Any type of raw meat, as long as it comes from a reliable source, will do, including beef, lamb, hog, chicken, rabbit, venison, tripe, and squirrel.
- Add the grated veggie or process it in your food processor. Any vegetable will do; however, raw potatoes are prohibited.
- Fresh produce should always be used. Vegetables really start to lose their nutritious value about a week after being harvested.
- Mix the ingredients thoroughly because some dogs have the same allergy to vegetables as a young child.
- Don't forget to get raw and meaty bones for your dog. These contain essential nutrients, promote healthy teeth, and keep their stools firm.
- If you are going to cook your own meals, you will probably discover that it saves you more time to prepare a fair amount in advance and freeze it. Shaping it into haphazard hamburgers or patties is a nice way to do this.

HOW MUCH TO SERVE?

To begin with, you will need to watch the quantity of food very carefully, but once you get the hang of it, you may do it by feel as long as your dog is about the right weight and appears healthy. Many effective raw feeders just keep a close eye on their pets and modify the quantity as needed.

There is no strict guideline, but for a dog weighing more than 10 kg, a daily food intake of about 2% of their body weight (including edible bones) should be adequate. In other words, a 20 kg dog should consume about 400g per day. This amount should be increased to between 2 and 5% of body weight each day if you have a working dog, a dog that is underweight, or a dog that exercises a lot. Reduce the quantity to between 1 and 2% of body weight daily if your dog is older or overweight.

However, it should never be left down for the dog to eat whenever they feel like it. You can offer it in as many meals as you wish and at any time. You might be shocked to know that wolves require almost three times the amount of food as an average dog due to their intense physical activity.

Try these for dogs under 11 kg:

- 1–2 kg : 10% of their weight
- 3–4 kg : 7% of their weight
- 5–8 kg : 5% of their weight
- 9–10 kg : 3% of their weight
- 11 kg+ : 2% of their weight

Note: These figures are provided merely as a guide.

HOW WILL YOU KNOW IF YOUR DOG HAS A NORMAL WEIGHT?

It's crucial for dogs to maintain a healthy body weight if they want to live an active and healthy life, and it's your duty as a dog owner to make sure they do. The results of a rigorous study carried out by Purina Pet Food and skilled animal nutritionists in 2002 demonstrated that dogs might live over two years longer by consuming a well-managed diet, compared to the usual canine lifespan of between ten and thirteen years. Helping your dog maintain a healthy weight has obvious advantages, but how do you tell if your dog is the right weight?

There are a few simple ways to evaluate whether your dog needs to adjust their way of life if you are concerned that they are underweight or overweight. If you would need a precise answer to this question, however, you can speak with a veterinarian or pet nutritionist.

Profile Analysis
A dog's abdomen should typically be higher than its ribcage, with the underside gradually sloping upward from the front legs to the rear. While a weak gradient or no incline at all implies that your dog is overweight, a severe slope indicates that your pet is underweight.

The ideal approach to examine your dog's profile is to stoop down until you are level with it, then turn to look at it from the side.

Rib Examination
Putting your hands open over your dog's ribs and both thumbs on its spine will allow you to readily determine if your dog is overweight.

You must be able to feel your pet's ribs under their coat and skin if they are a healthy weight, but if they are obese, you won't be able to. Check with your hands as well as your eyes because a dog's coat can easily conceal its ribs.

Horizontal Inspection
If you stand directly in front of a dog's face and look down, you should be able to notice that it has a form resembling an hourglass when it has a healthy body weight.

Its waist should ideally be visible tucked beneath the ribs. Your dog is underweight if you can see the shape of each individual rib, and the waist is noticeably smaller than the ribcage. On the other hand, if the waist is in line with the ribs or extends past them, your pet is overweight.

Whether your dog is overweight or underweight, you should change its lifestyle accordingly. If your pet is underweight, you can be over-exercising it and feeding it food with less calories. In this situation, a specifically formulated working dog food would be great because it is made to give dogs a sufficient amount of energy and also contains a variety of vitamins and minerals that will help them regain a healthy weight while also increasing their physical output.

On the other hand, if your dog is overweight, you should continue by increasing its daily exercise regimen and changing its diet to one that includes mostly of light dog food. Now is the moment for dog owners to aggressively combat canine obesity, as nearly half of the dogs in the US were reported to be overweight by veterinarians in 2014. If you notice that particular foods seem to upset your dog's stomach, try feeding your dog grain-free dog food to see if it helps with digestion and reduces bloating.

STORAGE GUIDELINES FOR HOMEMADE DOG FOOD

To guarantee that the meat is fully cooked when making your own dog food from cooked ingredients, heat the food to an internal temperature of 74 degrees Celsius. When you've finished preparing a batch of fresh food, you can either freeze it for up to six months or keep it in the freezer for roughly four days.

Use the same safety measures when serving freshly produced dog food as when serving canned dog food.

Keep dog treats fresh.

Treats are a wonderful method to express your affection for your dog or to praise positive behavior in him. But nobody, not even your dog, wants a stale and mushy treat. Take the following actions to keep treats pleasant and fresh:

- Keep treats at temperatures below 22 degrees Celsius
- Store opened bags of treats inside their original bags inside an airtight container or resealable plastic bag.
- Many treats are packaged in resealable bags to maintain freshness, which is crucial for soft treats. For maximum freshness, it's ideal for keeping freshly baked treats for your dog in the refrigerator in a container or bag that can be sealed. If soft treats are not kept in an airtight bag or container they may harden.

Preserving raw dog food appropriately.

There are crucial considerations for safely keeping your dog's raw food diet. When left at room temperature, raw meat can quickly go rancid.

- Always place covered containers of raw pet food in the refrigerator for not more than four days at a time.
- Use freezer-safe containers or resealable plastic bags to store food that is prepared in large quantities. If the frozen food is adequately secured from freezer burn, it can last for up to six months.
- When giving your dog food, make sure he consumes the entire portion in one sitting. If not, take the food right away and put any leftovers in the fridge. At room temperature, raw meat shouldn't be left out for longer than two hours at a time.
- Due to its propensity to spoil, never serve raw meat, even in timed feeders, throughout the day with a cooled compartment.

- Always wash your hands thoroughly after handling any kind of dog food, particularly raw meat.

The next chapter talks about special diet needs, such as recipes for dogs with allergies or medical conditions.

CHAPTER THREE

SPECIAL DIET NEEDS

When a chronic condition is identified in your pet, their once-favorite diet may no longer be effective for them. In certain instances, their usual diet might have even made them sick.

By switching to a special diet created for their health condition, they may find relief from their symptoms and even see a slowdown in the course of their illness. Your pet may not require as much reliance on prescription medications with the proper dietary support, though you should always see your veterinarian before modifying their dosage.

REASONS YOUR PET MAY NEED SPECIAL DIET

Like humans, pets are impacted by what they consume. While it is true that all pets should be provided with the healthiest food possible, there are instances when it is necessary to put them on a specific diet. We'll go over some of the causes of this possibility in this chapter.

Your Dog Has Allergies

It is likely that your pet has an allergy if they have had persistent scratching, redness, and in extreme circumstances, edema. As blood tests are not considered to be very accurate for detecting sensitivities, your veterinarian may advise that you do a food trial during which you need to remove the foods that might have been the source of your pet's allergy.

Eggs, wheat, dairy products, maize, and chicken are some of the foods that canines are usually sensitive to or allergic to, and these are often the main ingredients in dog food recipes. If you find that your pet has improved after a minimum of three weeks, your vet's nutritional counselor might recommend a diet to help you understand your pet's needs.

Achalasia of the Gland

Dogs have two tiny glands, known as anal sacs that emit a distinct aroma when they pass feces, alerting other animals that this is their territory. These sacs are often affected, irritated, or infected. As a result, abscesses can grow and burst, causing excruciating discomfort for your pet. To help your pet express these glands during excretion and avoid the various issues outlined above, you can give them a high-fiber diet.

Cancer

Even when their food consumption might otherwise be deemed acceptable, pets with cancer can lose weight. They often lose the same amount of muscle and fat, and when they experience decreased hunger, this process may be accelerated. The food that your pet consumes at this time can have an impact on their quality of life and likelihood of survival, so it is advised that you give your dog energizing meals that are high in fat and protein and low in carbohydrates.

Age Increase

A dog becomes a senior when he reaches the last third of his typical life expectancy, and this varies for each animal based on breed and species. As dogs age, they often suffer degenerative disorders like arthritis, which makes it harder for them to fall asleep. It is suggested that older dogs receive food that is richer in fiber and fewer in calories, as well as a supplement.

Obesity

Many dogs become accustomed to consuming excessive amounts of their own food or high-calorie table food, which causes them to gain weight. Pet owners have two options: they can construct a homemade diet or buy commercially available food that will sate their pet's desire while providing them with fewer calories. Whatever strategy is employed, it is imperative to raise the food's fiber content while lowering its fat content.

UNDERSTANDING FOOD ALLERGIES IN DOGS

A food allergy is one of the most frequent allergies or hypersensitivities that can affect dogs. The immune system of an allergic pet overreacts and produces antibodies to substances that it would not do otherwise. Antibodies are created in a food allergy to a particular dietary ingredient, usually a protein or complex carbohydrate. Food allergies often manifest after repeated exposure to a single brand, kind, or form of food since they require the production of antibodies in order to develop.

What medical symptoms do dogs with food allergies show?

Hives on paws, skin, or ears, as well as stomach problems like vomiting or diarrhea, are typical signs of a dog's food allergy. Other, more subtle changes including hyperactivity, weight loss, weariness, and even aggression may also appear.

What ingredients may trigger allergies?

The most common dietary allergies in dogs are triggered due to proteins, especially those derived from beef, dairy, chicken, soy, chicken eggs, or wheat gluten. These antigens and antibodies interact when a dog eats food containing them, leading to symptoms of food allergies. Practically, the ingredients in almost all foods, however, have the potential to trigger allergies. Proteins are usually one of them, although other substances and additives might also be the cause of some food allergy.

How are food allergies diagnosed?

The most accurate technique to identify a food allergy is through an elimination trial, in which routine food is replaced with other dog food for eight to twelve weeks. If you want this diet to be a true elimination trial for your dog, it cannot contain any foods that it has previously consumed. Additionally, it forbids the feeding of any additional foods, snacks, or supplements during the trial period, including flavored vitamins and certain parasite preventives.

If your dog's allergy symptoms go away while being treated with the food trial, the next step is to perform a food challenge by reintroducing your dog's old diet. Your dog's food allergy has been definitively identified if the symptoms go away after the food trial and return within a week of a subsequent food challenge.

Blood tests can be carried out to determine whether a dog is allergic to a given dish or not. These so-called serum IgE tests will be discussed with your pet's veterinarian to see if they can be used to diagnose your pet's condition. According to several researches, food exclusion tests may not be as successful as these blood tests are.

READING A DOG FOOD LABEL

Reading the label is one way to differentiate a bad dog food from a good one. This is easier said than done because large bags of dog food can be awkward to handle in stores, and labels can be difficult to see because of the small print. Labels, though, can often be deceptive. The Food and Drug Administration (FDA) mandates that dog food labels provide eight essential details, and individual states/provinces may also have their own labeling laws:

• Product name
• Net weight
• Manufacturer's name and address

- Guaranteed analysis
- Ingredients list
- Statement of nutritional adequacy
- Statement of intended animal species (e.g., dog or cat)
- Feeding guidelines

BEST DOG FOODS FOR DIFFERENT BREEDS

Dogs of different breed sizes require different types of nutrition. Large-breed dogs may require large-breed dog food with different nutrient balances to support musculoskeletal health, especially as puppies, because they are more prone to musculoskeletal issues than smaller breeds. While small-breed dogs have unique nutritional needs that can be accommodated with small-breed dog food that otherwise can choke on large-sized kibble. Investigate the breed of your dog to see if it has any particular nutritional requirements.

The next chapter talks about the use of supplements and additives in homemade dog food including the benefits and risks of using these ingredients.

CHAPTER FOUR

SUPPLEMENTS AND ADDITIVES

Homemade dog foods can pose the risk of nutritional deficiencies. Are dog supplements really essential? Almost all commercial dog foods are prepared with supplements. However, dealing with dog supplements for homemade dog food might be a little challenging.

The need of a homemade dog food recipe for essential dog vitamins mostly depends upon your dog and the recipe itself. Some recipes will also take into account any health problems your dog may have.

It is quite uncommon for homemade recipes to provide all the vitamins and minerals a dog requires in their ingredients. The majority of recipes may not contain the substantial ingredients, and it is not always clear what recipe has which ingredients. To shed some light on this crucial component of the homemade diet, it therefore important to give sufficient guidance on dog supplements for dog food.

CONVENTIONAL DOG SUPPLEMENTS

Nowadays, many dog owners give their dogs nutritional supplements. Currently, dogs with ailments and aged ones benefit from these dog supplements.

To ensure that the right nutrients are administered, it is usually advisable to talk to your veterinarian beforehand. Popular dog supplements and their purposes are listed below:

Dog probiotics

Probiotics are supplements for dogs that boost their immune systems, aid digestion, and combat infections. Additionally, probiotics create vitamins and nutrients that can benefit the microbiome of the dog. Health problems like diarrhea, allergies, obesity, and cramps may arise as their microbiota changes.

Fish Oil

Second, fish oil is one of the most well-liked dog supplements. EPA/DHA and omega-3 fatty acids are both present in this supplement.

Fish oil for dogs is available as a liquid or a pill. Since some dogs don't particularly enjoy ingesting tablets, the liquid form is typically easier to handle than the capsule.

A few more advantages of fish oil for dogs include the following:
- Protects the heart
- Great for a dog's coat
- Reduces anxiety
- Helps the dog's eyesight
- Helps arthritic joints
- Boosts the immune system
- Controls diabetes.

Antioxidants

Antioxidants are supplements for dogs that help prevent cellular damage. Additionally, it helps in reducing the consequences of ongoing inflammation.

However, a lack of antioxidants in your dog's diet can result in a variety of health issues, including heart disease, arthritic joints, skin allergies, respiratory illnesses, and eye and eyelid issues.

Glucosamine

Glucosamine is one of the most popular—if not the most—over-the-counter arthritic medications. As dogs are more prone to developing arthritis as they get older, Glucosamine aids in the reduction of hip dysplasia-related pain. Also, it aids in the treatment of spinal disc damage. Additionally, glucosamine supplements help speed up the healing of cartilage injuries.

WHY HOMEMADE DOG FOOD NEEDS SUPPLEMENTS?

Even the best dog food recipes suggested by vets and canine nutritionists don't always provide dogs with the necessary amounts of vitamins and minerals. Depending on the ingredients used, each homemade dog food recipe is unique and contains a diverse range of vitamins and minerals.

What dog supplements you'll need to add to your homemade dog chow depends on two things:

- Nutritional deficiencies in the recipe's ingredients
- The specific requirements and present health of your dog

In a 2013 study, 200 homemade dog food recipes from the UC Davis School of Veterinary Medicine were studied and compared. The 34 diverse sources for the recipes included pet care manuals, websites, and even veterinary textbooks. The ingredients and preparation of these recipes were examined by researchers and the findings indicated that only nine out of these 200 recipes met the minimum requirements specified by the Association of American Feed Control Officials for adult dogs (AAFCO). Out of these nine recipes only 5 recipes that fulfilled AAFCO minimal guidelines also contained the necessary nutrients in amounts appropriate for adult dogs, as determined by the National Research Council (NRC). Resultantly, the AAFCO and the NRC posited that only 2.5% of the 200 recipes studied provided adult dogs with the necessary nutrients.

Difficulty in Adding Supplements to Homemade Dog Food

It does not matter whether you choose a recipe from our list of the best ones at the end of this book or obtain one that your veterinarian suggests, they might not be completely nutritionally balanced. The majority of them will contain an adequate ratio of calories to macronutrients (protein, fat, and carbohydrates) but not to vitamins and minerals.

Every recipe's ingredients contain vitamins and minerals. You'll need to add dog food supplements to bring the ratio of calories to macronutrients to that ideal level that meets the requirements of your dog's diet plan. This implies that you must familiarize yourself in advance with the nutritional needs of your dog and the recommended serving sizes for homemade food. You can add supplements based on that.

Choosing multivitamin supplements for dogs can be challenging. For example, you are feeding your dog a meal that already provides all the calcium it requires. A dog who receives a multivitamin supplement with excessive calcium may eventually experience calcium poisoning (or hypercalcemia, a condition that can occur in dogs who take supplements).

On the other hand, if you opt not to add any dog food supplements to a homemade dog food recipe that isn't completely nutritionally balanced, your dog may become nutritionally deficient.

It is important to note that there is no single answer to a question like, "What dog supplement do I need to add to homemade dog food?" There are too many variables, so you'll have to determine what to do based on your own circumstances.

Here is How to Pick the Best Dog Supplements for Homemade Dog Food:

• Recognize your dog's specific calorie, macronutrient, and

micronutrient requirements (vitamins and minerals). To analyze your dog and assist you in calculating these statistics, it is recommended to ask a veterinarian or canine nutritionist. Put them in writing and keep them close.

- Pick a list of homemade dog food recipes that, as closely as possible, satisfy your pet's dietary requirements (ideally, show it to your vet).
- Determine which nutrients are entirely absent from those recipes or where their RDA values fall short of what your dog requires.
- Buy all the required dog supplements in accordance with those figures, and then add them to the recipe to make up for the deficient micronutrients while being cautious not to add too much.

The initial stages of this may seem difficult, and it does take some extra work, but if you get through them, you won't have to do it again (unless your dog's health condition changes).

You can pick from a wide variety of probiotic supplements and popular canine vitamins as long as you are aware of all those numbers.

WHAT TO CONSIDER BEFORE USING SUPPLEMENTS?

Consulting a canine nutritionist or veterinarian who is knowledgeable (not all vets are) about canine nutrition is the safest approach to do this effectively. Discuss with them your dog's specific nutritional needs, the dog supplements you can use in homemade dog food, and their recommended dosage.

The most typical dog supplements that are suggested for inclusion in home-cooked dog food recipes are:
- Hip and joint supplements

- Multivitamin supplements
- Omega-3 essential fatty acids (fish oil)
- Protein supplements
- Calcium
- Vitamins A & E

THINGS TO AVOID WHILE MAKING HOMEMADE DOG FOOD

It might be challenging to make homemade dog foods that provide a well-balanced diet. There are still many factors to take into account when making them.

You would need to be attentive and consistent when preparing a homemade dog food regimen. Here is a list of things to avoid while creating homemade dog food because we all want the best for our pets:

- Unhealthy Ingredients
- Inconsistent Recipe
- Overfeeding
- Using untrusted brands

ALWAYS MAKE ADJUSTMENTS WHEN NEEDED

Even when you've calculated the precise amounts and your recipes are now entirely well-balanced, you might occasionally need to make little changes.

The nutrients your dog's body requires from a meal each day and what you must add to your homemade dog foods depend on a variety of factors. It primarily relies on the age, breed, weight, environment, amount of exercise, past medical history, and present state of health of your dog.

For instance, if your dog has just been diagnosed with a condition, you will need to make changes to both the dog food supplements you feed your pet and the meals you give them.

The way you prepare and store that homemade dog food will also have an impact on the nutrients present in the recipe, in addition to the ingredients utilized.
For instance, essential nutrients may be destroyed when certain homemade dog diets are heated and frozen. You may determine all the dog nutrients needed for homemade dog food by conducting some research and arithmetic.

It is strongly advised to consult a canine nutritionist about your pet's homemade diet, even if you have the time to complete all of this research on your own.

You can protect yourself with only one consultation, and it's the only way to be certain that your dog is receiving the nourishment it needs.

In the next chapter, it you will find how to monitor your dog's health, including information on signs of good health, common health problems, and when to seek veterinary care.

CHAPTER FIVE

MONITORING YOUR DOG'S HEALTH

You want to do your best to ensure that your dog enjoys a healthy and long life since it is your baby (ideally forever).

Dogs make wonderful family pets. They always seem upbeat and entertaining to be around. But how can you spot a health issue in your dog?

Animals are unable to communicate with us about their health or level of pain. We must therefore keep an eye out for any warning indications that may point to a health problem in them. Here is some advice on how to examine your dog's health from head to tail at home. But first, why is it crucial to constantly keep an eye on your dog's health?

WHY SHOULD PET DOG'S HEALTH BE MONITERED?

Making sure your pet is healthy and content is one of your main duties as a dog owner. Monitoring your dog's health is essential to preserving their wellbeing because any problems may be quickly identified and treated, saving time and money. Here are a few explanations on why keeping an eye on your dog's health is so crucial.

- Early health condition detection: By keeping a regular eye on your dog's health, you can identify any problems before they become serious. This is essential for ensuring that your dog gets the proper care as soon as possible. Early diagnosis of health issues can also improve the likelihood of a full recovery, lessen the severity of the issue, and stop it from getting worse or even becoming life-threatening.

- Maintaining a healthy weight: Keeping your dog at a healthy weight is essential because being overweight or underweight can cause a number of health issues. You can keep an eye on your dog's weight to make sure that they are keeping a good body condition and, if necessary, make dietary or exercise changes.

- Observing their behavior: Observing your dog's behavior might help you spot any changes that might be signs of a health issue. For instance, if your dog starts to shun their favorite activities, gets more lethargic, or displays indications of discomfort, these could be early indicators of an issue that needs to be treated.

- Keeping an eye on their diet: Your dog's entire health and well-being depend on you feeding them a balanced, nutritious diet. It is possible to prevent health issues, maintain a healthy weight, and make sure your dog is getting all the nutrients they require by keeping an eye on their diet and adjusting it as needed.

- Preventing the transmission of diseases: Keeping an eye on your dog's health on a regular basis will aid in stopping the spread of illnesses and parasites. You may take action to ensure your dog receives fast treatment and stop the problem from spreading to other pets by spotting any problems early on.

Maintaining your dog's health and happiness requires constant attention. You can see any problems early on and take steps to stop them from getting worse by keeping an eye on your child's weight, behavior, nutrition, and general well-being. You can keep your dog healthy and content by giving them routine check-ups at the vet, keeping an eye on their behavior, and giving them a balanced and nourishing diet. As a result, be careful to keep a close eye on your dog and often check on their health. Your dog will appreciate it!

SIGNS OF GOOD HEALTH

A long and happy life is largely dependent on being in good health. So, how do we know the health of our dogs? They are unable to communicate their feelings to us, so we must rely on their outward behaviors to learn whether they are healthy and content or unwell. You can find your dog's eight most crucial health indicators below. Make a routine where you keep an eye out for these signals to help you spot any changes in your dog. Signs of good health include:

1. A healthy physique

Body weight is a crucial measure of health due to the impact it has on everything from joints to organs to general well-being.
When viewed from above, a dog's shape will be widest about the shoulders and narrow toward the hips. The smallest region of your dog's body should be the waist. There shouldn't be any bones, like the ribs, visible. However, you should be feel the ribs under the skin while caressing the sides, the ribcage.

Your dog's tummy should be seen from the side, but the ribs shouldn't be visible. The body contour of overweight dogs will be rounder, with a small waist or, in extreme situations, no waist at all. It will be required to feel for ribs and hip bones in dogs with thick coats of fur to make sure they are neither protruding nor covered by an excessive amount of fat.

2. Healthy drinking and eating habits

A healthy dog will consume enough water and have a suitable appetite for its age and level of exercise. A warning indicator that something is wrong is when your dog's food and drinking habits suddenly change without accompanying changes in activity levels. Loss of appetite is a general indication that your dog is ill, which means it could be a sign of many different illnesses and ailments. When discomfort, nausea, vomiting, diarrhea, or weakness are present, a vet should be called right away; likewise, if your dog starts consuming too much water.

3. A pleasant smell

- **Breathe:** A healthy mouth will have white, clean teeth and a neutral odor. Bad breath may be an indicator of a gastrointestinal issue, something caught in your dog's teeth, or an infection of the mouth. Since an infection in the mouth can spread to your dog's essential organs if left untreated, oral health is crucial for overall health. When you brush your dog's teeth, look for plaque, oral illness, or broken teeth.

- **Skin and coat:** Your dog's body odor shouldn't be overpowering when it's clean. One or more of the following conditions can be indicated by offensive body odor: allergies, impacted or inflamed anal sacs, skin conditions, or urinary tract infections. One of the most evident indicators of a dog's health is the state of its skin and coat. A dog with a healthy coat will be glossy and thick. They won't have dry or overly oily skin symptoms. One of the first indications that something is off is when the coat starts to lose its luster or turns dull or if you notice dandruff. It might indicate, for instance, a deficiency in micronutrients (such as omega 3, vitamin B, zinc, etc.). A balanced diet that contains healthy fatty acids will support healthy skin and fur.

- **Ears:** A dog's ears should not be overly waxy and should have a neutral smell. Additionally, your dog shouldn't be continuously itching to scratch them. Make it a practice to regularly smell your dog's ears to instantly spot any changes. Long-eared dogs are more likely to get ear problems.

4. Normal bowel movements

Looking at your dog's feces might reveal a lot about what is going on inside its body. The frequency of their bowel movements and the state of their poop or feces are reliable indicators of the caliber of their diet and digestive system. Brown, log-shaped, and firm (but not hard) feces is the indication of good gut health. It should be the right size for how much your dog consumes, be easy to pick up, and leave little or no waste on the ground. Gut health is improved with consuming canine kibble that contains probiotics and nutritious fiber.

5. A chilly, moist nose

The nose and/or snout should be wet and cold. A dry, cracked nose may indicate a fever or dehydration. A keratin-containing protein can be found on your dog's nose. It can occasionally grow too quickly, leading to a dry, crusty nose. You should take your dog's temperature via the rectum to check if it has a fever. Between 38.3 and 39.2 degrees in Celsius is considered normal.

6. Clearly pristine eyes

Healthy eyes will have pink inner lids and be bright and clear. A small amount of mucus, especially in the morning, is normal (but it should be minimal). A lot of eye discharge, red eyes, or hazy eyes in your dog are often symptoms of an infection or disease. If your dog has excessive cholesterol, you might even be able to know because one indication is hazy eyes and white patches. If your pet displays any of these symptoms, you should take him to the doctor right away: unusual eye discharge, swollen/red eyelids, itchy eyes, growths, or different-sized pupils. Diabetes and excessive sun exposure both have the potential to produce cataracts. Cataracts appear as a grey or opaque color on the eye.

7. Activity level and movement

The amount of energy your dog has should be appropriate for its age. Although puppies sleep a lot, they have a lot of energy when they are awake and ready to play. Due to their decreased energy levels, senior dogs need shorter walks more often. However, when moving, your senior dog shouldn't exhibit signs of suffering. The symptoms of pain, such as limping, stiffness, or an abnormal stride, include arthritis or an accident.

8. Calm and cheerful

Your dog's personality and mood are known to you, and healthy dogs typically maintain a steady mood. A well-socialized dog won't bite and will enjoy spending time with its family. It may be a symptom of pain or illness if your dog exhibits abrupt changes in mood or behavior, such as withdrawing or becoming irritable, or aggressive. A sudden shift in mood or personality may also be a sign of dementia or psychological trauma, fear, or stress.

COMMON HEALTH PROBLEMS

Some health issues, such as breathing difficulties for dogs with flat faces, are unique to certain breeds. However, all dogs are susceptible to a number of different health problems. Below are ten common health issues you should look out for in your canine companion:

Skin Issues

Itching is one of the most obvious indications that your dog has a skin issue. Rashes, redness, dry skin, lumps, pimples, skin sores, dandruff, and hair loss are further signs that your dog may have a skin condition.

Ear Conditions

Dogs who have ear problems account for about 20% of all cases. Breeds with floppy ears, like basset hounds and cocker spaniels, are especially prone to it. Wax buildup or discharge in their ear canal is common. Others, however, might feel discomfort, itching, redness, swelling, and crusting in their ears.

Infections of the Urinary Tract

This infection sometimes referred to as Urinary Tract Infection (UTI) can make it difficult for your beloved pet to pass urine. Drinking more water than normal and passing urine more often than usual are symptoms of a urinary tract infection. Additionally, your dog could pass very little waste or lose bladder control. Additionally, you can detect a strong scent in their urine or see blood in it.

Vomiting

Your pet could vomit for a variety of causes. You don't need to take your dog to the vet every time he throws up. But you can't ignore it either; that much is true. Try not to speculate. You must visit the veterinarian right once if the vomiting continues or happens along with other symptoms like diarrhea or weakness. It could be a symptom of serious health issues, like poisoning or a blockage in the digestive tract.

Diarrhea

This symptom could show up on its own or together with vomiting. Similar to vomiting, it could have comparable causes. A pet's diarrheal episode or episodes may not be life-threatening. However, persistent diarrhea might cause dehydration.

Parasites

At any time during their lifetime, your pet could feel discomfort due to internal or external parasites. The signs and symptoms of parasites might vary depending on a number of different things. These factors include the type of parasite that has afflicted your pet, its habitat, and the extent of its infestation.

Dental Problems

If there are too much plaque buildup, canine dental problems can harm your dog just like they can humans. There are a few symptoms - issues with chewing, gum or tooth bleeding, loose teeth, and foul breath - that suggest your pet may have dental disease.

Obesity

The general dog population is considered to be nearly 30% obese. A pet's obesity is influenced by a number of variables. Age, genetic predisposition, inactivity, and overeating are a few of these.

Arthritis

Your dog's mobility may be hampered by this joint condition. Take your dog to the veterinarian if he limps or becomes less active before and after walks. Other symptoms include behavioral changes and licking or chewing on sore spots.

Poisoning

The signs of dog poisoning might vary significantly depending on the sort of toxin that the dog has been exposed to. The symptoms can include drooling, vomiting, respiratory issues, seizures, or, even worse, coma. Foods that are consumed by humans, such as chocolate, grapes, raisins, onions, and caffeine, are among the most common toxic substances. Human prescription drugs, common cleaning supplies, insecticides, and some plants are further known offenders.

In such emergency, your pet dog depends on your ability to spot the first indications of problems and take quick action.

TIPS FOR MONITORING YOUR DOG'S HEALTH

Here are some tips to help you to keep track of your dog's ongoing health. When a health problem arises, early action can significantly impact healing and generally enhance the quality of life.

Drinking and eating

The majority of dogs have a predictable appetite that you can get used to. Similar to this, without a valid reason—such as hot weather or a change in diet—daily water intake shouldn't vary significantly. Your dog may occasionally decide to eat grass. While this activity might be normal on its own, it may need to be checked out if it is also accompanied by other symptoms.

The feces should be well-formed and free of any mucus or blood stains.

If your dog experiences diarrhea that lasts for longer than two days, it may require medical attention, especially if he has become out of sorts. The quality of the diet has a big impact on how much flatulence and how much feces are produced. Keep an eye out for bottom scooting, which is typically an indication of a worm infestation or an excessive buildup of fluid in the anal smell glands.

The coat should be thick, high-quality, and flake-free.

There shouldn't be any indication of significant coat thinning, patchiness, or skin inflammation. There are nutritional supplements available to help with improving the condition of the skin and coat. Quality food may make coats shine! Additionally, keeping an eye out for ticks and fleas is crucial. Monthly applications of highly efficient spot-on preventative preparations are available.

Ears

Ears should be odor-free and spotless. Lift the ear flap often to check for wax buildup or irritation. Periodic cleaning with a wax-eliminating solution can be required. Some breeds require frequent removal of extra hair from the ear canals. There are also 'spot on' products that are quite good at preventing ear mites.

Eyes

Eyes should be sparkling and brilliant, without any discharge or light sensitivity. Some breeds may experience routine tear overflow or a buildup of mucus at the corner of the eyes as a result of conformation defects. Smooth lid borders and a white appearance to the eye should be present. In case you are unsure, consult a veterinarian.

Nose
A clean, moist, smooth nose should not have any ulcerations or accumulations of discharge. There shouldn't be any persistent coughing, wheezing, or sneezing. Due to their conformation, some breeds are more likely to snore and snort. In case you are unsure, consult a veterinarian.

Teeth
Teeth should be routinely examined for plaque or tartar buildup. There shouldn't be a lot of bad breath coming from the mouth or lips, and the gums shouldn't appear irritated. To avoid periodontal disease and early tooth loss, many dogs require routine dental descaling at the veterinary clinic.

Nails
Nails should be examined for wear because if they grow out too long, they risk being ingrown or damaged. Don't forget to look at the dew claws, which are found on the inside surface of the foot higher up. A high-quality meal or nutritional supplement will typically increase the quality of your dog's nails.

Weight should be regularly checked.
You should be able to readily feel the ribs and see a clean waist from above. If a healthy pet follows the recommended food and exercise regimen, there is no good reason for them to become overweight. Neutering can occasionally make pets' metabolisms slower; thus, it's crucial to modify feeding amounts if body weight is rising. Additionally, we have prescription foods low in calories and fat, along with vitamins, to reduce hunger. Conditions including arthritis, heart failure, diabetes, liver failure, and breathing difficulties can all be brought on by or

made worse by obesity. Always keep up a healthy level of activity because diet alone cannot control weight.

Be alert for behavioral signs.
You know your pet! If they are off-form, they won't be as receptive as usual, be reluctant to get out of bed, have a hang-dog expression, be less tolerant of touch, be more clinging, etc.

WHEN TO SEEK VETERINARIAN CARE
Almost all veterinarians emphasize on a regular health and wellness checkup at least once a year. These appointments are important chances to monitor your pet's growth and nourishment, have your pet get a complete physical examination, and talk to your veterinarian about any worries you might have. Early symptoms of illness are often found during these visit checks as well, allowing them to be treated as soon as possible. When compared to addressing a fully formed medical issue that has already resulted in major problems, this can help the prognosis and result in lower veterinarian expenditures.

How can I know if my dog is in pain?
Dogs are inherently able to conceal any symptoms of discomfort. They inherited this instinct for self-preservation from their wild predecessors. However, if you do spend a lot of time with your dog, you will be able to detect even the minutest indications of pain.

The following are typical canine indications of pain:
- Crying
- Panting
- Reluctant to move or play
- Hunched over
- Shaking
- Loss of appetite
- Flattened ears
- Lameness

- Aggression
- Excessive licking or clawing at particular body parts

When should a dog that is vomiting be taken to the vet?
If your pet has been throwing up frequently during a day or for more than one day in consecutively, you should take him to the vet. If your dog is throwing up along with other symptoms, including lethargy, lack of appetite, diarrhea, blood in the stool or vomit, changes in water intake and urine, collapse, and abdominal pain, you should also seek medical attention.

When should I visit the veterinarian with my dog's itching?
Dogs with persistent itching should be seen by a veterinarian as soon as possible. Tears and fissures in the skin can eventually result from chewing and scratching, which can lead to a secondary bacterial infection. Additionally, excessive hair loss might result from severe itching. A trip to the vet can help in determining the underlying reason so that immediate treatment can be provided.

When should I take my dog to an emergency vet?
Even with routine health and wellness examinations performed annually or bi-annually, emergencies do happen. Knowing how to recognize critical symptoms can help you seek immediate veterinarian assistance, which is highly important during the first stages of a problem or condition. Visit the closest veterinary facility right away if your pet dog exhibits any of the following symptoms:

- Vomits blood
- Has experienced vomiting, diarrhea, or both for longer than 24 hours
- Passes blood in the stool
- Trauma, such as being struck by a car, falling from a great height, or being struck by a blunt object

- Experiences seizures
- Broken bones
- Breathing difficulty
- Unconsciousness
- Pale gums
- Has eaten something toxic, such as household cleaners, lawn, and garden products, antifreeze, rat/slug bait, etc.
- Showing symptoms of extreme pain
- Sudden collapse and inability to get up
- The abdomen feels hard to the touch or is bloated
- Appears disoriented

In the next chapter, you will be exposed to a variety of basic recipes for homemade dog food, including ingredients and instructions for making each recipe.

COOKING CONVERSION CHART

Table for Measurement Conversion

Volume/Liquied				Weight		Temperature	
Table-spoon (tbsp.)	Ounce (oz.)	Milli-liters (ml.)	Cup (c.)	Impe-rial	Metric	Fahren-heit (ºF)	Celsius (ºC)
1 tbsp.	1/2 oz.	15 ml.	1/16 c.	1/2 oz.	15 g	100º F	37º C
3 tbsp.	1 oz.	30 ml.	1/8 c.	1 oz.	29 g	150º F	65º C
4 tbsp.	2 oz.	59 ml.	1/4 c.	2 oz.	57 g	200º F	93º C
5.5 tbsp.	2.5 oz.	79 ml.	1/3 c.	3 oz.	85 g	250º F	121º C
6 tbsp.	3 oz.	90 ml.	3/8 c.	4 oz.	113 g	300º F	150º C
8 tbsp.	4 oz.	118 ml.	1/2 c.	5 oz.	141 g	325º F	160º C
11 tbsp.	5 oz.	158 ml.	2/3 c.	6 oz.	170 g	350º F	180º C
12 tbsp.	6 oz.	177 ml.	3/4 c.	8 oz.	227 g	375º F	190º C
16 tbsp.	8 oz.	240 ml.	1 c.	10 oz.	283 g	400º F	200º C
32 tbsp.	16 oz.	480 ml.	2 c.	12 oz.	340 g	425º F	220º C
64 tbsp.	32 oz.	960 ml.	4 c.	13 oz.	369 g	450º F	230º C
80 tbsp.	40 oz.	1180 ml.	5 c.	14 oz.	397 g	500º F	260º C
96 tbsp.	48 oz.	1420 ml.	6 c.	15 oz.	425 g	525º F	274º C
128 tbsp.	64 oz.	1895 ml.	8 c.	1 pound (lb.)	453 g	550º F	288º C

CHAPTER SIx

HOMEMADE DOG FOOD RECIPES

These recipes will show you how to prepare a delicious meal for your furry friend. It is made with a variety of nutritious and easily available ingredients that offer a healthful balance of nutrients.

Feeding your dog homemade dog food is one way to ensure that you are aware of everything that is in its bowl. If you have a picky dog, food sensitivities, or allergies, this is vitally important.

The 95 homemade dog food recipes covered in this chapter are essential for a balanced diet for dogs.

HEALTHY HOMEMADE DOG FOOD RECIPES

Recipe 1	Beef and Vegetable Stew

A warming stew that is ideal for your pet on a chilly day.

Ingredients:

- 1 cup chopped potatoes
- 1 cup diced carrots
- 1 cup beef broth
- 1 cup diced green beans
- 1 lb. ground meat

Macros

- 330 Calories
- 20 g fat
- 20 g carbohydrates
- 33 g protein

4 servings

Instructions:

1. Lightly brown the ground meat in a large pot over medium heat.
2. Add the diced potatoes, carrots, and green beans.
3. Boil the beef broth after adding it.
4. Reduce the heat to a simmer and cook the stew for 20 minutes or until the veggies are fork-tender.
5. Let it cool before feeding your dog the stew.

Comments:

Recipe 2	Chicken and Rice

A quick and wholesome dinner for your dog.

Ingredients:

- 1 cup frozen mixed vegetables (peas, corn, and carrots)
- 2 cups cooked and shredded chicken
- 2 cups brown rice

Macros

- 350 calories
- 40 g protein
- 10 g fat
- 40 g carbohydrates

4 servings

Instructions:

1. Follow the package instructions for cooking the brown rice.
2. Sauté frozen mixed vegetables in a different pan until they are soft.
3. In a sizable bowl, mix the cooked chicken, rice, and vegetables.
4. Serve your dog the mixture

Comments:

....

....

....

....

Recipe 3	Turkey and Sweet Potato

A dish that is high in protein and benefits from sweet potatoes.

Ingredients:

- 1 cup green beans
- 2 cup cooked and mashed sweet potatoes
- 2 cup cooked, shredded turkey

Macros

- 300 Calories
- 40 g protein
- 10 g fat
- 30 g carbohydrates

4 servings

Instructions:

1. Cook and mash the sweet potatoes.
2. Cook the green beans till they are cooked through.
3. Mix the cooked turkey, mashed sweet potatoes, and green beans in a big bowl.
4. Serve your dog the mixture.

Comments:

Recipe 4	Salmon and Broccoli

A nutrient- and Omega-3 fatty acid-rich dinner.

Ingredients:

- 2 cups of cooked salmon
- 1 cup of brown rice
- 2 cups of boiled broccoli

Macros

- 360 calories
- 40 g protein
- 20 g fat
- 20 g carbohydrates

4 servings

Instructions:

1. Follow the package instructions for cooking the brown rice.
2. Cook the broccoli only till it's soft.
3. Combine the cooked salmon, broccoli, and rice in a big bowl.
4. Serve your dog the mixture.

Comments:

....

....

....

....

| Recipe 5 | **Apples with Pork** |

A delicious dinner that is certain to please your pet.

Ingredients:

- 1 cup green beans
- 2 cups sliced apples
- 2 cups cooked and shredded pork

Macros

- 300 Calories
- 40 g protein
- 10 g fat
- 20 g carbohydrates

3 servings

Instructions:

1. Cook the green beans until they are cooked through.
2. Mix the cooked pork, apple slices, and green beans in a sizable bowl.
3. Serve your dog the mixture.

Comments:

....

....

....

....

Recipe 6	Lentil and Carrot

A meal high in protein with carrots for added health benefits.

Ingredients:
- 1 cup brown rice
- 2 cups cooked lentils
- 2 cups sliced carrots

Macros
- 300 Calories
- 30 g protein
- 5 g fat
- 40 g carbohydrates

4 servings

Instructions:
1. Follow the package instructions for cooking the brown rice.
2. Cook the diced carrots until they are soft.
3. Mix the cooked rice, carrots, and lentils in a sizable bowl.
4. Sever meal to your dog.

Comments:

....

....

....

....

Recipe 7	Beef and Carrot

A quick lunch that is nutrient-dense.

Ingredients:

- 1 cup brown rice
- 2 cups cooked and diced beef
- 2 cups diced carrots

Macros

- 300 calories
- 40 g protein
- 20 g fat
- 20 g carbohydrates

4 servings

Instructions:

1. Follow the package instructions for cooking the brown rice.
2. Cook the diced carrots until they are soft.
3. Mix the cooked beef, rice, and carrots in a sizable bowl.
4. Serve the meal to your dog

Comments:

....

....

....

....

Recipe 8	**Chicken and Quinoa**

A dish that is packed in protein and benefits from quinoa.

Ingredients:

- 1 cup frozen mixed vegetables (peas, corn, and carrots)
- 2 cups cooked and shredded chicken
- 2 cups cooked quinoa

Macros
- 300 calories
- 40 g protein
- 10 g fat
- 30 g carbohydrates

5 servings

Instructions:

1. Prepare the quinoa as directed on the package.
2. Cook the frozen mixed vegetables until they are soft.
3. In a big bowl, mix the cooked chicken, quinoa, and veggies.
4. Serve the meal to your dog

Comments:

....

....

....

....

Recipe 9	Turkey and Green Bean

A meal that is high in protein and has the advantages of green beans.

Ingredients:

- 1 cup brown rice
- 2 cups cooked and shredded turkey
- 2 cups cooked green beans

Macros

- 300 Calories
- 40 g protein
- 10 g fat
- 20 g carbohydrates

4 servings

Instructions:

1. Follow the package instructions for cooking the brown rice.
2. Cook the green beans till they are cooked through.
3. Mix the cooked turkey, green beans, and rice in a big bowl.
4. Serve the meal to your dog.

Comments:

....

....

....

....

Recipe 10	Salmon and Asparagus

A delicious and nutritious dinner that also has the advantages of asparagus.

Ingredients:

- 1 cup brown rice
- 2 cups cooked salmon
- 2 cups cooked asparagus.

Macros

- 300 calories
- 40 g protein
- 20 g fat
- 20 g carbohydrates

4 servings

Instructions:

1. Follow the package instructions for cooking the brown rice.
2. Continue cooking the asparagus until it is tender.
3. Mix the cooked salmon, asparagus, and rice in a big bowl.
4. Serve the meal to your dog.

Comments:

Recipe 11	Sweet Potato and Pork

A wonderful dinner packed with necessary nutrients.

Ingredients:

- 1 cup brown rice
- 2 cups cooked and diced sweet potato
- 4 cups cooked and diced pork

Macros

- 300 calories
- 30 g protein
- 20 g fat
- 25 g carbohydrates

4 servings

Instructions:

1. Follow the package instructions for cooking the brown rice.
2. Cook the diced sweet potatoes until they are cooked through.
3. Mix the cooked pork, sweet potato, and rice in a big bowl.
4. Serve the meal to your dog.

Comments:

....

....

....

....

Recipe 12	Lentil and Peas

A meal that is high in protein and has the advantages of peas.

Ingredients:
- 1 cup brown rice
- 2 cups cooked peas
- 2 cups cooked lentils

Macros
- 250 Calories
- 30 g protein
- 5 g fat
- 35 g carbohydrates

4 servings

Instructions:
1. Follow the package instructions for cooking the brown rice.
2. Cook the peas until they are soft.
3. Mix the cooked rice, peas, and lentils in a sizable bowl.
4. Serve the meal to your dog.

Comments:
....

....

....

....

Recipe 13

Sweet Potato and Beef

A healthy dinner with sweet potatoes' extra benefits.

Ingredients:

- 1 cup brown rice
- 2 cups cooked and diced beef
- 2 cups cooked and diced sweet potato

Macros
- 300 calories
- 40 g protein
- 20 g fat
- 25 g carbohydrates

4 servings

Instructions:

1. Follow the package instructions for cooking the brown rice.
2. Cook the diced sweet potatoes until they are cooked through.
3. Mix the cooked beef, sweet potato, and rice in a big bowl.
4. Serve the meal to your dog.

Comments:

....

....

....

....

Recipe 14

Chicken and Brown Rice

A quick and healthy food for your pet.

Ingredients:

- 1 cup frozen mixed vegetables (peas, corn, and carrots)
- 2 cups cooked and shredded chicken
- 2 cups brown rice

Macros
- 320 calories
- 40 g protein
- 10 g fat
- 30 g carbohydrates

4 servings

Instructions:

1. Follow the package instructions for cooking the brown rice.
2. Cook the frozen mixed vegetables until they are soft.
3. In a sizable bowl, mix the cooked chicken, rice, and vegetables.
4. Serve the meal to your dog.

Comments:

....

....

....

....

Recipe 15	Squash and Turkey

A meal that is high in protein and has the benefits of squash.

Ingredients:
- 1 cup brown rice
- 2 cups cooked and chopped squash
- 2 cups cooked and shredded turkey

Macros
- 300 Calories
- 40 g protein
- 10 g fat
- 25 g carbohydrates

4 servings

Instructions:
1. Follow the package instructions for cooking the brown rice.
2. Cook the squash until they are soft.
3. Mix the cooked turkey, squash, and rice in a sizable bowl.
4. Serve the meal to your dog.

Comments:
....
....
....
....

Recipe 16

Spinach and Salmon

A healthy dish with spinach's added benefits.

Ingredients:

- 1 cup brown rice
- 2 cups cooked spinach
- 2 cups cooked salmon

Macros
- 300 calories
- 40 g protein
- 20 g fat
- 20 g carbohydrates

4 servings

Instructions:

1. Prepare the brown rice following the instructions on the package.
2. Cook the spinach until it is soft.
3. Mix the cooked salmon, spinach, and rice in a big bowl.
4. Serve the meal to your dog.

Comments:

....

....

....

....

Recipe 17	**Pork and Green Beans**

Green beans give extra health advantages to this delectable dish.

Ingredients:

- 1 cup brown rice
- 2 cups cooked and chopped pork
- 2 cups cooked green beans

Macros

- 300 calories
- 30 g protein
- 20 g fat
- 25 g carbohydrates

4 servings

Instructions:

1. Follow the package instructions to cook the brown rice.
2. Cook the green beans till they are cooked through.
3. Mix the cooked pork, green beans, and rice in a big bowl.
4. Serve the meal to your dog.

Comments:

Recipe 18	Squash with Lentils

A meal that is high in protein and has the benefits of squash.

Ingredients:

- 1 cup brown rice
- 2 cups cooked lentils
- 2 cups cooked and diced squash

Macros

- 300 calories
- 30 g protein
- 5 g fat
- 35 g carbohydrates

4 servings

Instructions:

1. Follow the package instructions for cooking the brown rice.
2. Cook the squash until they are soft.
3. Mix the cooked lentils, squash, and rice in a big bowl.
4. Serve the meal to your dog.

Comments:

Recipe 19	Beef and Carrot

A healthy dish with carrots' extra benefits.

Ingredients:

- 1 cup brown rice
- 2 cups cooked and diced meat
- 2 cups cooked and diced carrots

Macros

- 300 calories
- 40 g protein
- 20 g fat
- 25 g carbohydrates

4 servings

Instructions:

1. Follow the package instructions for cooking the brown rice.
2. Cook the diced carrots until they are soft.
3. Mix the cooked beef, rice, and carrots in a sizable bowl.
4. Serve the meal to your dog.

Comments:

....

....

....

....

Recipe 20 — Butternut Squash and Chicken

A healthy meal with butternut squash's added benefits.

Ingredients:
- 1 cup brown rice
- 2 cups cooked and diced butternut squash
- 2 cups cooked and shredded chicken

Macros
- 305 calories
- 40 g protein
- 10 g fat
- 25 g carbohydrates

4 servings

Instructions:
1. Follow the package instructions for cooking the brown rice.
2. Cook the butternut squash in a pot until they are soft.
3. In a sizable bowl, mix the cooked chicken, squash, and rice.
4. Serve the meal to your dog.

Comments:
....
....
....
....

Recipe 21

Carrots with Turkey

A turkey and carrot recipe that is both delicious and nutritious.

Ingredients:
- 1 lb. boneless and skinless turkey
- 2 cups chopped carrots

Macros
- 303 calories
- 20 g protein
- 5 g fat
- 10 g carbohydrates

4 servings

Instructions:
1. Heat a large skillet.
2. Add the turkey to the skillet and cook it until both sides are browned.
3. Place the diced carrots in the skillet and cook through.
4. Serve the meal to your dog.

Comments:

....

....

....

....

Recipe 22	**Salmon and Carrot**

A simple recipe for a great and healthy meal.

Ingredients:

- 1 lb. salmon
- 2 cups chopped carrots

Macros

- 300 calories
- 20 g protein
- 5 g fat
- 10 g carbohydrates

4 servings

Instructions:

1. Heat a large skillet.
2. Add the salmon in the skillet and cook it through.
3. Place the diced carrots in the skillet and cook through.
4. Serve the meal to your dog.

Comments:

....

....

....

....

Recipe 23	Pork and Peas

A delicious and nutritious dish made with pork and peas.

Ingredients:
- 1 lb. skinless and boneless pork
- 2 cups frozen peas

Macros
- 300 calories
- 20 g protein
- 5 g fat
- 10 g carbohydrates

4 servings

Instructions:
1. Heat a large skillet.
2. Place the pork in the pan and heat until both sides are browned.
3. Add the frozen peas in the skillet and heat through.
4. Serve the meal to your dog.

Comments:

Recipe 24

Lentil and Carrot

A quick to prepare dish that is satisfying and nutritious.

Ingredients:
- 2 cups chopped carrots
- 1 cup lentils

Macros
- 200 Calories
- 10 g protein
- 2 g fat
- 20 g carbohydrates

4 servings

Instructions:
1. Wash the lentils and drain them.
2. Fill a pot with water and add the lentils and diced carrots.
3. After heating the pot, turn down the heat.
4. Cook the lentils and carrots for about 30 minutes, or until they are tender.
5. Give your dog the lentils and carrots.

Comments:

Recipe 25	**Beef and Broccoli**

A dish made with beef and broccoli that is delicious and nutritious.

Ingredients:

- 1 lb. skinless and boneless beef
- 2 cups chopped broccoli

Macros

- 300 calories
- 20 g protein
- 5 g fat
- 10 g carbohydrates

4 servings

Instructions:

1. Heat a large skillet.
2. Add the beef to the pan and heat until both sides are browned.
3. Place the chopped broccoli in the skillet and heat through.
4. Give your dog the steak and broccoli.

Comments:

....

....

....

....

Recipe 26

Sweet Potato and Chicken

A delicious and nourishing combo for your pet.

Ingredients:

- 1 lb. skinless and boneless chicken breast
- 2 cups chopped and diced sweet potatoes
- 2 tbsp. olive oil

Macros

- 305 calories.
- 50 g protein
- 10 g fat
- 20 g carbohydrates

4 servings

Instructions:

1. Set the oven to 400° F.
2. Put the sweet potatoes and chicken in a roasting dish.
3. After putting the meat to the skillet, drizzle with olive oil.
4. Bake the sweet potatoes and chicken for 25 to 30 minutes, or until the chicken is thoroughly cooked.
5. After cooling, serve it to your dog.

Comments:

....

....

....

....

Recipe 27

Rice and Turkey

A nutritious meal that is ideal for dogs that are allergic to chicken.

Ingredients:

- 1 cup uncooked white rice
- 2 tsp. olive oil
- 1 lb. ground turkey

Macros

- 300 Calories
- 40 g protein
- 20 g fat
- 30 g carbohydrates

4 servings

Instructions:

1. Cook rice as directed on the packet.
2. Heat the olive oil to medium heat in a separate pan.
3. Add the ground turkey and sauté it, breaking it up as it cooks, until it is browned.
4. Add the cooked rice to the browned turkey and mix thoroughly.
5. After cooling, serve it to your dog.

Comments:

Recipe 28

Rice and Salmon

A tasty and healthful alternative for fish-loving canines.

Ingredients:

- 2 tbsp. olive oil
- 1 cup uncooked white rice
- 1 lb. salmon fillets

Macros

- 300 Calories
- 40 g protein
- 20 g fat
- 20 g carbohydrates

4 servings

Instructions:

1. Prepare rice as directed on the packet.
2. Set the oven to 400° F.
3. Set salmon fillets in an oven-safe dish.
4. After putting the meat to the skillet, drizzle with olive oil.
5. Bake the salmon for 12 to 15 minutes, or until it is done.
6. Add flaked salmon to the cooked rice.
7. After it has cooled, serve it to your dog.

Comments:

Recipe 29

Pork and Sweet Potato

A delicious and nutritious dish that is ideal for dogs who want some diversity in their diet.

Ingredients:

- 1 lb. pork tenderloin
- 2 cups diced and peeled sweet potatoes
- 2 tsp. extra virgin olive oil

Macros
- 320 calories
- 40 g protein
- 20 g fat
- 20 g carbohydrates

4 servings

Instructions:

1. Set the oven to 400° F.
2. Put sweet potatoes and pork tenderloin in a baking dish.
3. After adding the pork to the skillet, drizzle with olive oil.
4. Bake for 25 to 30 minutes, or until sweet potatoes are soft and the pork is thoroughly cooked.
5. After cooling, serve it to your dog.

Comments:

....

....

....

....

Recipe 30	Lentil and Rice

A satisfying and nutritious dish that is ideal for dogs searching for a low-fat option.

Ingredients:

- 1 cup uncooked white rice
- 1 cup dried green lentils
- 2 tsp. olive oil

Macros

- 300 Calories
- 20 g protein
- 10 g fat
- 40 g carbohydrates

4 servings

Instructions:

1. Prepare rice and lentils as directed on the package.
2. Heat the olive oil to medium heat in a separate pan.
3. Add the cooked rice and lentils.
4. Mix thoroughly and let it to cool.
5. Serve the meal to your dog.

Comments:

....

....

....

....

Recipe 31	Beef and Rice

A traditional dish that is ideal for dogs who enjoy red meat.

Ingredients:

- 1 cup uncooked white rice
- 1 lb. ground beef
- 2 tsp. extra virgin olive oil

Macros

- 300 calories
- 40 g protein
- 20 g fat
- 30 g carbohydrates

4 servings

Instructions:

1. Prepare rice as directed on the packet.
2. Heat the olive oil to medium heat in a separate pan.
3. Add the ground beef and cook until it is browned.
4. Add the cooked rice and thoroughly mix.
5. After cooling, serve the meal to your dog.

Comments:

....

....

....

....

Recipe 32

Carrots and Chicken

A healthy meal that is ideal for dogs who enjoy vegetables.

Ingredients:

- 1 lb. skinless and boneless chicken breast
- 2 cups chopped and diced carrots
- 2 tbsp. olive oil

Macros

- 300 calories
- 50 g protein
- 10 g fat
- 20 g carbohydrates

4 servings

Instructions:

1. Set the oven to 400° F.
2. Fill a baking dish with the chicken and the vegetables.
3. After putting the meat to the skillet, drizzle with olive oil.
4. Bake the chicken for 25 to 30 minutes, or until it is thoroughly cooked, and the vegetables are soft.
5. After cooling, serve it to your dog.

Comments:

....

....

....

....

Recipe 33

Lentils and Turkey

A satisfying and nutritious meal that is ideal for dogs who need to increase their intake of fiber.

Ingredients:

- 1 cup dried green lentils
- 2 tsp. olive oil
- 1 lb. ground turkey

Macros

- 300 calories
- 40 g protein
- 20 g fat
- 20 g carbohydrates

4 servings

Instructions:

1. Prepare lentils as directed on the packaging.
2. Heat the olive oil to medium heat in a separate pan.
3. Add the ground turkey and cook it while breaking it up until it is browned.
4. Add the cooked lentils and thoroughly mix.
5. After cooling, serve this meal to your dog.

Comments:

....

....

....

....

Recipe 34

Lentils with Salmon

A delicious and nutritious meal that is ideal for dogs who enjoy fiber and fish.

Ingredients:

- 2 tsp. olive oil
- 1 cup dried green lentils
- 1 lb. salmon fillets

Macros

- 300 calories
- 40 g protein
- 20 g fat
- 20 g carbohydrates

4 servings

Instructions:

1. Prepare lentils as directed on the package.
2. Set the oven to 400° F.
3. Set salmon fillets in an oven-safe dish.
4. After putting the meat to the skillet, drizzle with olive oil.
5. Bake the salmon for 12 to 15 minutes, or until it is done.
6. Toss cooked lentils with flaked salmon.
7. After it has cooled, serve it to your dog.

Comments:

....

....

....

....

Recipe 35

Pork and Lentils

A delicious and nutritious dish that is ideal for dogs who want some diversity in their diet.

Ingredients:

- 1 cup dried green lentils
- 1 lb. ground pork
- 2 tsp. olive oil

Macros

- 310 calories
- 40 g protein
- 20 g fat
- 20 g carbohydrates

4 servings

Instructions:

1. Prepare lentils as directed on the package.
2. Heat the olive oil to medium heat in a separate pan.
3. Add the ground pork and cook it while breaking it up until it is browned.
4. Add the cooked lentils and thoroughly mix.
5. After cooling, serve it to your dog.

Comments:

....

....

....

....

QUICK AND EASY HOMEMADE DOG RECIPES

Recipe 36	Chicken and Brown Rice Bake

A quick and healthy one-pan meal for your pet.

Ingredients:

- 1 cup brown rice
- 1 lb. boneless and skinless chicken breast
- 2 cups water
- 2 cups mixed vegetables (e.g., carrots, peas, corn)

Macros
- 200 calories
- 35 g protein
- 5 g fat
- 40 g carbohydrates

4 servings

Instructions:

1. Set the oven to 375° F.
2. Combine the chicken, brown rice, water, and mixed vegetables in a sizable baking dish.
3. Cover the dish with foil and bake it for 45 minutes.
4. Take off the foil and bake for an additional 10-15 minutes, or until the rice and chicken are cooked through.
5. Serve the meal to your dog.

Comments:

....

....

....

....

Recipe 37	Ground Beef and Vegetable Stir Fry

A flavorful and nutritious stir-fry dish that will delight your dog's palate.

Ingredients:

- 2 cups mixed vegetables, such as broccoli, bell peppers, and carrots
- 1 tbsp. olive oil
- 1 lb. ground beef

Macros

- 200 calories
- 35 g protein
- 20 g fat
- 10 g carbohydrates

4 servings

Instructions:

1. In a big skillet, warm the olive oil.
2. Add the ground beef and sauté it until it is browned.
3. Stir-fry the mixed vegetables for 5-7 minutes, or until they are soft.
4. Serve the meal to your dog

Comments:

Recipe 38	Turkey and Sweet Potato Skillet

A quick and easy to prepare meal that is filling and healthy for your pet.

Ingredients:
- 1 lb. ground turkey
- 2 cups diced sweet potatoes
- 1 tbsp. olive oil

Macros
- 200 calories
- 35 g protein
- 10 g fat
- 20 g carbohydrates

4 servings

Instructions:
1. In a big skillet, warm the olive oil.
2. Add the ground turkey and heat it until it is browned.
3. Stir-fry the diced sweet potato for 5-7 minutes, or until it is cooked.
4. Serve the meal to your dog.

Comments:
....
....
....
....

Recipe 39	Quick Salmon and Vegetable Bake

A flavorful and fast meal that is packed with nutrients.

Ingredients:

- 1 lb. diced salmon fillet
- 2 cups mixed vegetables, such as broccoli, bell peppers, and carrots
- 1 tbsp. olive oil

Macros

- 200 calories
- 35 g protein
- 15 g fat
- 10 g carbohydrates

4 servings

Instructions:

1. Set the oven to 375° F.
2. Mix salmon, mixed vegetables, and olive oil in a sizable baking dish.
3. Bake the salmon and vegetables for 15 to 20 minutes, or until the fish is cooked through.
4. Serve the meal to your dog.

Comments:

....

....

....

....

| Recipe 40 | **Pork and Apple Sauté** |

A delicious and nutritious meal that is sure to suit your dog's palate.

Ingredients:
- 2 cups chopped apples
- 1 tbsp. olive oil
- 1 lb. ground pork

Macros
- 200 Calories
- 35 g protein
- 20 g fat
- 10 g carbohydrates

4 servings

Instructions:
1. In a big skillet, warm the olive oil.
2. Add the ground pork and sauté it until it is browned.
3. Stir-fry the diced apples for 5–7 minutes, or until they are soft.
4. Serve the meal to your dog.

Comments:
....
....
....
....

Recipe 41 — Instant Pot Lentil and Chicken

A simple and quick dinner prepared in an Instant Pot for your pet.

Ingredients:
- 1 cup green lentils
- 1 lb. boneless and diced chicken breast
- 2 cups water
- 1 tbsp. olive oil

Macros
- 200 calories
- 35 g protein
- 5 g fat
- 20 g carbohydrates

4 servings

Instructions:
1. Fill an Instant Pot with all the ingredients and stir to mix.
2. Cover the Instant Pot, then cook for 20 minutes at manual high pressure.
3. Quickly let the pressure out.
4. Serve the meal to your dog.

Comments:
....

....

....

....

Recipe 42

Beef and Veggie Bowl

A quick and healthy meal for your animal companion.

Ingredients:
- 2 cups of mixed vegetables, such as broccoli, bell peppers, and carrots
- 1 tbsp. olive oil
- 1 lb. of ground beef

Macros
- 250 Calories
- 35 g protein
- 20 g fat
- 10 g carbohydrates

4 servings

Instructions:
1. In a big skillet, warm the olive oil.
2. Add the ground meat and sauté it until it is browned.
3. Stir-fry the mixed vegetables for 5-7 minutes, or until they are soft.
4. Serve the meal to your dog.

Comments:
....
....
....
....

Recipe 43	Chicken and Rice Casserole

A hearty, simple casserole that's ideal for a comforting meal.

Ingredients:
- 1 cup white rice
- 1 lb. diced boneless chicken breast
- 2 cups water
- 2 cups mixed vegetables (e.g., carrots, peas, corn)

Macros
- 200 calories
- 35 g protein
- 5 g fat
- 40 g carbohydrates

4 servings

Instructions:
1. Set the oven to 375° F.
2. Mix the chicken, white rice, water, and mixed vegetables in a sizable baking dish.
3. Cover the dish with foil and bake it for 45 minutes.
4. Take off the foil and bake for an additional 10 to 15 minutes, or until the rice is tender and the chicken is fully cooked.
5. Serve the meal to your dog.

Comments:

Recipe 44

Quick Turkey and Rice Bowl

An ideal fast and simple meal for those hectic weekdays.

Ingredients:
- 1 cup white rice
- 2 cups water
- 1 tbsp. olive oil
- 1 lb. ground turkey

Macros
- 200 calories
- 35 g protein
- 10 g fat
- 20 g carbohydrates

4 servings

Instructions:
1. Boil water in a big pot.
2. Add the white rice and cook it for 18 to 20 minutes, or until it is tender.
3. Heat the olive oil in a different skillet over medium-high heat.
4. Add the ground turkey and cook it until it is browned.
5. Place the browned turkey on top of the cooked rice.
6. Serve the meal to your dog.

Comments:

....

....

....

....

Recipe 45 — One Pot Salmon and Veggies

A quick and healthy one-pan dinner for your pet.

Ingredients:
- 1 lb. diced salmon fillet
- 2 cups mixed vegetables, such as broccoli, bell peppers, and carrots
- 1 tbsp. olive oil

Macros
- 200 calories
- 35 g protein
- 15 g fat
- 10 g carbohydrates

4 servings

Instructions:
1. Set the oven to 375° F.
2. Mix the salmon pieces, mixed vegetables, and olive oil in a sizable baking dish.
3. Toss everything to evenly distribute the oil over the vegetables and salmon.
4. Bake for 20 to 25 minutes, or until the vegetables are soft and the salmon is cooked.
5. Serve the hot meal to your dog.

Comments:
....
....
....
....

VEGAN/VEGETARIAN HOMEMADE DOG FOOD RECIPES

Recipe 46	Sweet Potato and Peanut Butter

A tasty and sweet meal for your animal companion.

Ingredients:

- 1 cup water
- 2 tbsp. peanut butter
- 1 large sweet potato

Macros

- 300 calories
- 12 g fat
- 10 g protein
- 40 g carbohydrates

2 servings

Instructions:

1. Peel the sweet potato after washing it.
2. Chop the sweet potato into tiny pieces.
3. Boil it in a pot of water for about 10 minutes, or until the sweet potato is tender.
4. Remove the sweet potato from the water and mash it in a bowl.
5. Add the peanut butter and thoroughly mix.
6. Serve the meal to your dog.

Comments:

....

....

....

....

Recipe 47

Carrot and Quinoa Bowl

A healthy and well-balanced meal for your dog.

Ingredients:

- 2 carrots
- 1 cup quinoa
- 2 cups water

Macros

- 250 calories
- 6 g fat
- 8 g protein
- 40 g carbohydrates

2 servings

Instructions:

1. Quinoa should be rinsed before being put in a pot.
2. Put water inside it and boil.
3. Reduce the heat and cover the pot.
4. To fully cook the quinoa, cook for 20 minutes.
5. Slice the peeled and washed carrots into small pieces.
6. In a pot of water, boil the carrots for 10 minutes or until they are tender.
7. Remove the carrots from the water and mash them in a bowl.
8. In a bowl, mix the cooked quinoa and mashed carrots.
9. Serve the meal to your dog.

Comments:

....

....

....

....

Recipe 48 — Green Bean and Rice Bowl

A delicious and nutritious meal for your pet.

Ingredients:
- 2 cups water
- 1 cup green beans
- 1 cup brown rice

Macros
- 300 calories
- 6 g fat
- 8 g protein
- 50 g carbohydrate

2 servings

Instructions:
1. Place the rice in a pot after rinsing.
2. Boil it after adding the water.
3. Reduce the heat and cover the pan with a lid.
4. It takes the rice about 20 minutes to fully cook.
5. Green beans should be washed and trimmed.
6. Boil the green beans in a pot of water for 10 minutes, or until they are tender.
7. Remove the green beans from the water and mash them in a bowl.
8. In a bowl, mix the mashed green beans and cooked rice.
9. Serve the meal to your dog.

Comments:

....

....

....

....

Recipe 49	Spinach and Chickpea Casserole

A delicious and nutritious casserole for your pet.

Ingredients:

- 2 cups spinach
- 1 cup water
- 1 cup chickpeas

Macros

- 250 calories
- 6 g fat
- 10 g protein
- 30 g carbohydrate

2 servings

Instructions:

1. Rinse and drain the chickpeas.
2. After washing, cut the spinach into small pieces.
3. In a casserole dish, mix the spinach and chickpeas.
4. Add the water and wrap the foil around it.
5. Bake for 20 minutes, or until it's thoroughly heated.
6. Serve the meal to your dog.

Comments:

....

....

....

....

Recipe 50

Broccoli and Brown Rice

A delicious and nutritious meal for your pet.

Ingredients:

- 2 cups broccoli florets
- 1 cup brown rice
- 2 cups water

Macros

- 300 Calories
- 6 g fat
- 8 g protein
- 50 g carbohydrate

2 servings

Instructions:

1. Put the rice in a pot after rinsing.
2. Boil it after adding the water.
3. Reduce the heat and cover the pan with a lid.
4. It takes the rice about 20 minutes to fully cook.
5. Cut the broccoli into small pieces after washing.
6. In a casserole dish, mix the cooked rice and broccoli.
7. Bake the dish for 20 minutes or until it's thoroughly heated at 350°F. Wrap in foil.
8. Serve the meal to your dog.

Comments:

....

....

....

....

Recipe 51

Squash and Lentil Skillet

A delicious and nutritious meal for your pet.

Ingredients:

- 2 cups squash
- 1 cup lentils
- 2 cups water

Macros

- 250 calories
- 6 g fat
- 10 g protein
- 30 g carbohydrates

2 servings

Instructions:

1. The lentils should be rinsed and drained.
2. Squash should be cleaned and cut into small pieces.
3. The lentils and squash should be added to a skillet and heat.
4. Add the water, then cover with a lid.
5. To fully cook the lentils and squash, cook for 20 minutes.
6. Serve the meal to your dog.

Comments:

Recipe 52	Sweet Potato and Black Bean Bowl

A healthy and well-balanced meal for your dog.

Ingredients:

- 1 large sweet potato
- 1 cup of black beans
- 2 cups of water

Macros

- 300 calories
- 6 g fat
- 50 g carbohydrates
- 10 g protein

2 servings

Instructions:

1. Wash and drain the black beans before cooking.
2. Peel the sweet potato after washing it.
3. Peel and chop the sweet potato into tiny pieces.
4. To cook the sweet potato, place it in a pot of water and boil it.
5. Remove the sweet potato from the water and mash it in a bowl.
6. Mix mashed sweet potato and black beans in a bowl.
7. Serve the meal to your dog.

Comments:

....

....

....

....

Recipe 53

Carrot and Tofu Casserole

A delicious and nourishing casserole for your pet.

Ingredients:

- 2 carrots
- 2 cups water
- 1 cup tofu

Macros

- 250 calories
- 6 g fat
- 8 g protein
- 30 g carbohydrates

2 servings

Instructions:

1. Drain the tofu and crumble it.
2. Slice the peeled and washed carrots into small pieces.
3. In a pot of water, boil the carrots for 10 minutes or until they are soft.
4. Drain the water, and in a bowl, mash the carrots.
5. Toss the mashed carrots and crumbled tofu together in a casserole dish.
6. Add the water and wrap the foil around it.
7. Bake for 20 minutes, or until well heated.
8. Serve the meal to your dog.

Comments:

Recipe 54

Green Bean and Lentil Bake

A wonderful and scrumptious food for your pet.

Ingredients:

- 2 cups water
- 1 cup lentils
- 1 cup green beans

Macros

- 250 calories
- 6 g fat
- 10 g protein
- 30 g carbohydrates

2 servings

Instructions:

1. Wash the lentils and drain them.
2. Also wash the green beans are trimmed them.
3. Boil the green beans in a pot of water for 10 minutes or until they are cooked.
4. Remove the green beans from the water and mash them in a basin.
5. In a casserole dish, mix the lentils and mashed green beans.
6. Add the water and wrap the foil around it.
7. Bake for 20 minutes, or until it's well heated.
8. Serve the meal to your dog.

Comments:

....
....
....
....

Recipe 55 — Spinach and Rice Casserole

A delicious and nutritious food for your pet.

Ingredients:

- 2 cups fresh spinach
- 1 cup brown rice
- 2 cups water

Macros

- 300 calories
- 6 g fat
- 8 g protein
- 50 g carbohydrates

2 servings

Instructions:

1. Put the rice in a pot after rinsing.
2. Boil it after adding water.
3. Reduce the heat and cover the pan with a lid.
4. It takes the rice around 20 minutes to thoroughly cook.
5. Prepare the spinach for chopping.
6. In a casserole dish, mix the cooked rice and spinach.
7. Bake the dish for 20 minutes or until it's well cooked at 350°F.
8. Wrap with foil.
9. Serve the meal to your dog.

Comments:

....

....

....

....

KETO HOMEMADE DOG FOOD RECIPES

Recipe 56	Chicken and Cauliflower Rice

A nutritious and tasty meal for your pet!

Ingredients:
- 2 cups chopped cauliflower
- 1 lb. diced boneless chicken breast
- 2 tbsp. olive oil
- Pepper and salt to taste

Macros
- 337 calories
- 16 g fat
- 36 g protein
- 10 g carbs

4 servings

Instructions:
1. Turn a large skillet to medium heat.
2. Fill the skillet with olive oil.
3. Add salt and pepper to the skillet before adding the diced chicken.
4. Cook for 7 to 10 minutes, or until the chicken is browned.
5. Stir the chicken and chopped cauliflower together in the skillet.
6. Continue to cook the cauliflower for a further 7 to 10 minutes, or until it's soft.
7. Serve the meal to your dog.

Comments:

Recipe 57	Beef and Broccoli Stir Fry

A quick and delicious meal for your dog.

Ingredients:

- 2 cups broccoli florets
- 1 lb. chopped beef
- 2 tbsp. olive oil
- Salt and pepper to taste

Macros

- 384 calories
- 25 g fat
- 32 g protein
- 7 g carbs

4 servings

Instructions:

1. Put a large skillet to medium heat.
2. Fill the skillet with olive oil.
3. Add salt and pepper to the skillet before adding the diced beef.
4. Cook for 7 to 10 minutes, or until the beef is browned.
5. Stir the beef and broccoli florets together in the skillet.
6. Continue to cook the broccoli for a further 5-7 minutes, or until it's soft.
7. Serve the meal to your pet dog.

Comments:

....
....
....
....

Recipe 58

Turkey and Zucchini Skillet

A healthy and low-carb meal for your pet.

Ingredients:

- 2 tbsp. extra virgin olive oil
- 2 medium zucchinis
- 1 lb. ground turkey
- Pepper and salt to taste

Macros
- 314 calories
- 17 g fat
- 32 g protein
- 9 g carbs

4 servings

Instructions:

1. Put a large skillet to medium heat.
2. Fill the skillet with olive oil.
3. Add salt and pepper to the ground turkey before placing it into the skillet.
4. Cook for 7 to 10 minutes, or until the turkey is browned.
5. Add the zucchini in the skillet and swirl it into the turkey mixture.
6. Cook the zucchini for a further 5-7 minutes, or until it is soft.
7. Serve the meal to your pet dog.

Comments:

....

....

....

....

Recipe 59	Pork and Butternut Squash Salad

A porky meal with a mixture of butternut squash which is rich and flavorful meal for your dog.

Ingredients:

- 1 lb. ground pork
- 1 bowl butternut squash (peeled and diced)
- 1 bowl minced kale
- 1 bowl minced green beans
- 1 tbsp. coconut oil
- 2 cups water

Macros

- 365 Calories
- 14 g fat
- 32 g carbs
- 23 g protein

3-4 servings

Instructions:

1. In a huge pot, set the coconut oil over medium heat.
2. Place the ground pork and cook until browned, stirring occasionally.
3. Add the butternut squash, kale, green beans, and water to the pot.
4. When the mixture boils down, reduce heat to low and simmer for 20-25 minutes or until the vegetables are tender.
5. Let it cool.
6. Serve it to your pet dog.

Comments:

....

....

....

Recipe 60	**Pork and Brussels Sprout Casserole**

A wonderful and scrumptious meal for your pet!

Ingredients:

- 2 cups chopped Brussels sprouts
- 1 lb. sliced pork tenderloin
- 2 tbsp. extra virgin olive oil
- Salt and pepper to taste

Macros
- 377 calories
- 17 g fat
- 42 g protein
- 14 g carbohydrates

4 servings

Instructions:

1. Put a large skillet to medium heat.
2. Fill the skillet with olive oil.
3. Add salt and pepper to the skillet before adding the diced pork.
4. Cook for 7 to 10 minutes, or until the pork is browned.
5. Stir in the chopped Brussels sprouts with the pork in the skillet.
6. Cook the Brussels sprouts for an additional 5-7 minutes, or until they are soft.
7. Serve the meal to your pet dog.

Comments:

Recipe 61 — Chicken and Spinach Casserole

A nutritious and tasty meal for your pet.

Ingredients:
- 1 lb. diced boneless chicken breast
- 2 cups fresh spinach
- 2 tbsp. olive oil
- Salt and pepper to taste

Macros
- 325 calories
- 14 g fat
- 39 g protein
- 9 g carbohydrates

4 servings

Instructions:
1. Put a large skillet to medium heat.
2. Fill the skillet with olive oil.
3. Add salt and pepper to the skillet before adding the diced chicken.
4. Cook for 7 to 10 minutes, or until the chicken is browned.
5. Add the spinach in the skillet and stir it into the chicken mixture.
6. Continue cooking for an additional 2 to 3 minutes, or until the spinach is wilted.
7. Serve the meal to your dog.

Comments:
....
....
....
....

Recipe 62

Beef and Green Bean Bake

A wonderful and scrumptious meal for your pet!

Ingredients:
- 1 lb. diced beef
- 2 cups fresh green beans
- 2 tbsp. olive oil
- Salt and pepper to taste

Macros
- 380 calories
- 25 g fat
- 32 g protein
- 11 g carbohydrates

4 servings

Instructions:
1. Put a large skillet to medium heat.
2. Fill the skillet with olive oil.
3. Add salt and pepper to the skillet before adding the diced beef.
4. Cook for 7 to 10 minutes, or until the beef is browned.
5. Stir in the fresh green beans after you've added the steak to the skillet.
6. Cook the green beans for an additional 5-7 minutes, or until they are soft.
7. Serve the meal to your pet dog.

Comments:

....

....

....

....

Recipe 63 — Turkey and Cauliflower Bake

A nutritious and low-carb dinner for your pet.

Ingredients:
- 2 cups chopped cauliflower
- 1 lb. ground turkey
- 2 tbsp. olive oil
- Salt and pepper to taste

Macros
- 337 calories
- 16 g fat
- 36 g protein
- 10 g carbs

4 servings

Instructions:
1. Put a large skillet to medium heat.
2. Fill the skillet with olive oil.
3. Add salt and pepper to the skillet before adding the ground turkey.
4. Cook for 7 to 10 minutes, or until the turkey is browned.
5. Stir the turkey and chopped cauliflower together in the skillet.
6. Continue to cook the cauliflower for a further 5-7 minutes, or until it gets tender.
7. Serve the meal to your pet dog.

Comments:
....
....
....
....

Recipe 64 — Salmon and Broccoli Casserole

A delicious and healthy meal for your pet.

Ingredients:

- 2 cups chopped broccoli
- 1 lb. diced salmon
- 2 tbsp. of olive oil
- Salt & pepper to taste

Macros

- 397 calories
- 23 g fat
- 41 g protein
- 11 g carbs

4 servings

Instructions:

1. Put a large skillet to medium heat.
2. Fill the skillet with olive oil.
3. Add salt and pepper to the skillet before adding the diced salmon.
4. Cook for 7 to 10 minutes, or until the salmon is browned.
5. Add the chopped broccoli in the skillet with the salmon and swirl to incorporate.
6. Continue to cook the broccoli for a further 5-7 minutes, or until it's soft.
7. Serve the meal to your pet dog.

Comments:

....

....

....

....

Recipe 65

Pork and Zucchini Skillet

A wonderful and scrumptious meal for your pet.

Ingredients:

- 1 lb. diced pork tenderloin
- 2 cups sliced zucchini
- 2 tbsp. extra virgin olive oil
- Salt and pepper to taste

Macros
- 337 calories
- 17 g fat
- 42 g protein
- 11 g carbs

4 servings

Instructions:

1. Put a large skillet to medium heat.
2. Fill the skillet with olive oil.
3. Add salt and pepper to the skillet before adding the diced pork.
4. Cook for 7 to 10 minutes, or until the pork is browned.
5. Stir the meat and diced zucchini together in the skillet.
6. Cook the zucchini for a further 5-7 minutes, or until it is soft.
7. Serve the meal to your pet dog.

Comments:

....

....

....

....

WEIGHT GAIN/WEIGHT LOSS HOMEMADE DOG RECIPES

Recipe 66	Chicken and Vegetable Soup for Weight Loss

A healthy soup with less calories to aid with dog weight loss.

Ingredients:

- 1 lb. cubed, boneless and skinless chicken breast
- 2 cups carrot, celery, and onion
- 4 cups low-sodium chicken broth

Macros

- 140 calories
- 25 g protein
- 3 g fat
- 6 g carbs

6 servings

Instructions:

1. In a big pot, soften the vegetables by sautéing them.
2. Place the chicken in the pan and heat it through, making sure the meat is no longer pink.
3. Add the chicken broth and fully heat.
4. Reduce the heat and simmer the food for 20 minutes.
5. Serve the hot meal to your pet dog.

Comments:

....

....

....

....

Recipe 67	Beef and Cauliflower Skillet for Weight Gain

A meal high in protein and calories to aid in dog weight gain.

Ingredients:

- 1 lb. ground beef
- 1 chopped cauliflower
- 2 tbsp. of olive oil

Macros

- 400 calories
- 25 g protein
- 30 g fat
- 10 g carbs

4 servings

Instructions:

1. Get a skillet and heat the olive oil.
2. Add the ground beef and cook until it is browned.
3. Add the chopped cauliflower into the skillet and cooked through.
4. Serve the hot meal to your pet dog.

Comments:

....

....

....

....

Recipe 68
Turkey and Sweet Potato Casserole for Weight Gain

A nourishing casserole with lots of calories to help dogs put on weight.

Ingredients:
- 1 lb. ground turkey
- 2 cups diced sweet potatoes
- 1 tbsp. olive oil

Macros
- 400 calories
- 25 g protein
- 25 g fat
- 25 g carbs

4 servings

Instructions:
1. Set the oven to 375° F.
2. In a pan, heat the olive oil.
3. After adding the ground turkey, cook until it gets brown.
4. Place the sweet potatoes in a roasting dish with the turkey.
5. Bake the sweet potatoes for 25 minutes, or until they are tender.
6. Serve the hot meal to your pet dog.

Comments:

Recipe 69	Salmon and Asparagus Bake for Weight Loss

A healthy meal with few calories to aid in weight loss in dogs.

Ingredients:

- 2 cups chopped asparagus
- 1 tbsp. olive oil
- 1 lb. salmon fillet

Macros

- 200 calories
- 25 g protein
- 10 g fat
- 6 g carbs

4 servings

Instructions:

1. Set the oven to 375° F.
2. Warm up the olive oil in a skillet.
3. Place the salmon fillet in the pan and cook for 3 minutes on each side.
4. Place the chopped asparagus with the fish in a baking tray.
5. Bake for 15 minutes, or until the salmon is fully cooked and the asparagus is soft.
6. Serve the hot meal to your pet dog.

Comments:

....

....

....

....

Recipe 70
Pork and Green Bean Casserole for Weight Gain

A meal high in protein and calories to aid in dog weight gain.

Ingredients:
- 1 lb. chopped pork chops
- 2 cups green beans
- 2 tbsp. olive oil

Macros
- 400 calories
- 25 g protein
- 30 g fat
- 10 g carbs

4 servings

Instructions:
1. Get a skillet and heat the olive oil in it.
2. Add pork chops that have been diced and cooked till they are browned.
3. Add the green beans and keep cooking until they are tender.
4. Serve the hot meal to your pet dog.

Comments:
....
....
....
....

Recipe 71 | Chicken and Broccoli Bake for Weight Loss

A healthy meal with few calories to aid in weight loss in dogs.

Ingredients:

- 1 lb. cubed skinless and boneless chicken breast
- 2 cups broccoli florets
- 1 tbsp. olive oil

Macros

- 200 calories
- 25 g protein
- 10 g fat
- 6 g carbs

4 servings

Instructions:

1. Set the oven to 375° F.
2. In a pan, heat the olive oil.
3. Stir in the cubed chicken, and heat it until the color is gone.
4. Add the broccoli florets and transfer the chicken to a baking dish.
5. Bake for 15 minutes, or until the chicken is cooked through and the broccoli is soft.
6. Serve the hot meal to your pet dog.

Comments:

Recipe 72

Beef and Carrot Casserole for Weight Gain

A meal high in protein and calories to aid in dog weight gain.

Ingredients:

- 1 lb. ground beef
- 2 cups sliced carrots
- 2 tbsp. olive oil

Macros

- 400 calories
- 25 g protein
- 30 g fat
- 10 g carbs

4 servings

Instructions:

1. In a pan, heat the olive oil.
2. Add the ground beef and cook it in the pan until it is browned.
3. Add the diced carrots and continue cooking until they are tender.
4. Serve the meal to your pet dog.

Comments:

....

....

....

....

Recipe 73	Turkey and Zucchini Stir Fry for Weight Loss

A healthy meal with few calories to aid in weight loss in dogs.

Ingredients:

- 2 cups chopped zucchini
- 1 tbsp. olive oil
- 1 lb. ground turkey

Macros

- 200 calories
- 25 g protein
- 10 g fat
- 6 g carbs

4 servings

Instructions:

1. In a pan, heat the olive oil.
2. Add the ground turkey and heat it until it is browned.
3. Add the diced zucchini and keep cooking until it softens.
4. Serve the meal to your pet dog.

Comments:

....

....

....

....

Recipe 74 | Salmon and Spinach Bake for Weight Loss

A healthy meal with few calories to aid in weight loss in dogs.

Ingredients:
- 1 lb. salmon fillet
- 2 cups spinach
- 1 tbsp. olive oil

Macros
- 200 calories
- 25 g protein
- 10 g fat
- 6 g carbs

4 servings

Instructions:
1. Set the oven to 375° F.
2. Heat the olive oil in a skillet.
3. Place the salmon fillet in the pan and cook for 3 minutes on each side.
4. Place the chopped spinach alongside the fish in a baking tray.
5. Bake the salmon for 15 minutes, or until it is done.
6. Serve the hot meal to your pet dog.

Comments:

....

....

....

....

Recipe 75	**Pork and Brussels Sprout for Weight Gain**

A meal high in protein and calories to aid in dog weight gain.

Ingredients:
- 2 cups chopped Brussels sprouts
- 1 lb. diced pork chops
- 2 tbsp. olive oil

Macros
- 400 calories
- 25 g protein
- 30 g fat
- 10 g carbs

4 servings

Instructions:
1. In a pan, heat the olive oil.
2. Add pork chops that have been diced and cook till it is browned.
3. Stir in the chopped Brussels sprouts, and simmer for another minute or two until it is tender.
4. Serve the hot meal to your pet dog.

Comments:
....
....
....
....

TREATS AND DESSERTS
HOMEMADE DOG RECIPES

Recipe 76	Peanut Butter Banana Bites

A tasty and easy dog treat.

Ingredients:
- 2 tbsp. peanut butter
- 1 ripe banana

Macros
- 120 calories
- 6 g fat
- 15 g carbs
- 3 g protein

Makes approximately 12 bites.

Instructions:
1. Set oven temperature to 350° F. Use parchment paper to cover a baking sheet.
2. Mash the banana in a bowl
3. Add the peanut butter and mix thoroughly.
4. Scoop out 12 balls of the mixture with a cookie scoop, and place them on the preheated baking sheet.
5. Bake for 15 to 20 minutes, or until it turns golden and firm.
6. Allow it to cool completely.
7. Then, serve the meal to your pet dog.

Comments:
....
....
....
....

Recipe 77	Sweet Potato Chews

These chewy, crispy snacks are nutrient- and fiber-rich.

Ingredients:
- 1 medium sweet potato

Macros
- 60 calories
- 0 g fat
- 15 g carbohydrates
- 2 g protein

Makes approximately 6 to 8 chews.

Instructions:
1. Set oven temperature to 250° F. Use parchment paper to cover a baking sheet.
2. Slice the peeled and washed sweet potato into thin rounds.
3. Spread out the slices in a single layer on the baking sheet that has been warmed.
4. Bake the slices for two to three hours, or until they are totally hard and dry.
5. Allow it to cool completely.
6. Then, serve it to your pet dog.

Comments:
....
....
....
....

Recipe 78

Carrot and Apple Treats

These tasty and crunchy candies are loaded with vitamins and antioxidants.

Ingredients:
- 1 medium apple
- 2 medium grated carrots

Macros
- 60 calories
- 0 g fat
- 15 g carbohydrates
- 1 g protein

Yields 12 to 14 treats.

Instructions:
1. Set oven temperature to 350° F. Use parchment paper to cover a baking sheet.
2. Mix the grated apples and carrots in a bowl.
3. Using a cookie scoop, shape the dough into 12 to 14 balls, then set the balls on the preheated baking sheet.
4. Bake for 20 to 25 minutes, until they get brown and firm.
5. Allow it to cool completely.
6. Then, serve it to your pet dog.

Comments:
....

....

....

....

Recipe 79 — Yogurt and Blueberry Drops

These probiotic- and antioxidant-rich frozen treats are ideal for a sunny day.

Ingredients:
- 1 cup plain yogurt
- 1/2 cup fresh blueberries

Macros
- 40 calories
- 2 g fat
- 5 g carbohydrates.
- 3 g protein

Makes approximately 12 drops.

Instructions:
1. Use parchment paper to cover a baking sheet.
2. Mix the yogurt and blueberries in a bowl.
3. Using a cookie scoop, shape the dough into 12 to 14 balls, then set the balls on the preheated baking sheet.
4. Freeze for at least two hours or until firm.
5. Keep the frozen treats in the freezer for two to three months in an airtight container.
6. Give this cool treat to your dog on a hot day.

Comments:
....
....
....
....

Recipe 80	Peanut Butter and Pumpkin Treats

These chewy and squishy snacks are a powerhouse of antioxidants and fiber.

Ingredients:

- 1 egg
- 1 cup pumpkin puree
- 1/2 cup peanut butter
- 1/2 cup oat flour

Macros

- 70 Calories
- 5 g fat
- 6 g carbohydrates
- 3 g protein

Around 20–24 treats

Instructions:

1. Set oven temperature to 350° F. Use parchment paper to cover a baking sheet.
2. In a bowl, mix the egg, oat flour, pumpkin puree, and peanut butter.
3. Using a cookie scoop, shape the dough into 12 to 14 balls, then set the balls on the preheated baking sheet.
4. Bake for 15 to 20 minutes, or until it becomes golden and firm.
5. Allow it to cool completely
6. Then, serve the meal to your pet dog.

Comments:

Recipe 81	Sweet Potato and Coconut Treats

These chewy and squishy snacks are stacked with fiber and good fats.

Ingredients:

- 1 mashed medium sweet potato
- 1/2 cup coconut flour
- 1/4 cup unsweetened coconut flakes
- 2 tsp. coconut oil
- 1 egg

Macros

- 60 calories
- 4 g fat
- 6 g carbohydrates
- 2 g protein

Yields 20 to 24 treats.

Instructions:

1. Set oven temperature to 350° F. Use parchment paper to cover a baking sheet.
2. Mix the mashed sweet potato, coconut oil, coconut flour, and shredded coconut in a bowl.
3. Using a cookie scoop, shape the dough into 12 to 14 balls, then set the balls on the preheated baking sheet.
4. Bake for 15 to 20 minutes, or until it turns golden and firm.
5. Allow it to cool completely.
6. Then, serve the meal to your pet dog.

Comments:

....

....

....

....

Recipe 82	**Carrot and Oat Cookies**

The amount of fiber and antioxidants in these chewy cum soft cookies is sufficient for your dog.

Ingredients:
- 2 grated medium carrots
- 1 cup oat flour
- 2 tbsp. peanut butter
- 1 egg

Macros
- 70 Calories
- 4 g fat
- 8 g carbohydrates
- 3 g protein

Makes approximately 20–24 cookies.

Instructions:
1. Set oven temperature to 350° F. Use parchment paper to cover a baking sheet.
2. Mix the grated carrots, oat flour, peanut butter, and egg in a bowl.
3. Using a cookie scoop shape the dough into 12 to 14 balls, then set the balls on the preheated baking sheet.
4. Bake for 15 to 20 minutes, or until it turns golden and firm.
5. Allow it to cool completely.
6. Then, serve it to your pet dog.

Comments:
....
....
....
....

Recipe 83 — Yogurt and Banana Treats

Probiotics and vitamins are abundant in these soft and chewy treats.

Ingredients:
- 1 mashed ripe banana
- 1 cup plain yogurt
- 1/2 cup oat flour

Macros
- 50 calories
- 2 g fat
- 8 g carbohydrates
- 3 g protein

Yields 20 to 24 snacks.

Instructions:
1. Set oven temperature to 350° F. Use parchment paper to cover a baking sheet.
2. Mix the yogurt, mashed banana, and oat flour in a bowl.
3. Using a cookie scoop shape the dough into 12 to 14 balls, then set the balls on the preheated baking sheet.
4. Bake for 15 to 20 minutes, or until it gets golden and firm.
5. Allow it to cool completely.
6. Then serve it to your pet dog.

Comments:
....
....
....
....

Recipe 84	**Peanut Butter and Sweet Potato Treats**

These treats are soft and chewy and loaded with vitamins and good fats.

Ingredients:
- 1 mashed medium sweet potato
- 1 cup peanut butter
- 1 egg
- 1/2 cup oat flour

Macros
- 70 Calories
- 5 g fat
- 6 g carbohydrates
- 3 g protein

Yields 20 to 24 treats.

Instructions:
1. Set oven temperature to 350° F. Use parchment paper to cover a baking sheet.
2. Mix the egg, mashed sweet potato, peanut butter, and oat flour in a bowl.
3. Using a cookie scoop shape the dough into 12 to 14 balls, then set the balls on the preheated baking sheet.
4. Bake for 15 to 20 minutes, or until it turns golden and firm.
5. Allow it to cool completely.
6. Then, serve it to your pet dog.

Comments:
....

....

....

....

Recipe 85	Carrot and Peanut Butter Biscuits

These salty and crispy biscuits are a great source of fiber and good fats.

Ingredients:

- 2 grated medium carrots
- 1 cup whole grain flour
- 2 tbsp. peanut butter
- 1 egg

Macros

- 70 Calories
- 4 g fat
- 8 g carbohydrates
- 3 g protein

Makes approximately 20–24 biscuits.

Instructions:

1. Set oven temperature to 350° F. Use parchment paper to cover a baking sheet.
2. Mix the egg, whole wheat flour, peanut butter, and grated carrots in a bowl.
3. Using a cookie scoop shape the dough into 12 to 14 balls, then set the balls on the preheated baking sheet.
4. Bake for 25 to 30 minutes, or until it turns golden and firm.
5. Allow it to cool completely.
6. Then, serve it to your pet dog.

Comments:

....

....

....

....

Recipe 86

Salmon and Quinoa

Gives you a loaded meal for our furry friends that are filled with protein and carbs.

Ingredients:

- 1 lb. boneless and skinless salmon fillet
- 1 bowl cooked quinoa
- 1 bowl minced green beans
- 1 bowl minced carrots
- 1 tbsp. coconut oil
- 2 cups water

Macros

- 375 Calories
- 15 g fat
- 32 g carbs
- 24 g protein

Makes 2-3 servings.

Instructions:

1. Set the oven to 400° F.
2. Place the salmon fillet on a baking sheet and bake for at least 12-15 minutes or until fully cooked.
3. In a huge container, put the coconut oil over mid-heat.
4. Put together the green beans, carrots, and water in the pot and bring them to a boil.
5. Decrease the heat to low and simmer for approximately ten to fifteen minutes or until the vegetables are tender.
6. Add the cooked quinoa and flaked salmon to the pot and stir until they are mixed thoroughly.
7. Let it cool down.
8. Then, serve it to your pet dog.

Comments:

Recipe 87 — Braised Beef and Sweet Potato

A flavorful food for our dogs that they will surely be joyful of.

Ingredients:
- 1 lb. ground beef
- 2 sweet potatoes (squared and peeled)
- 1 bowl minced spinach
- 1 bowl minced carrots
- 1 tbsp. olive oil
- 2 cups of water

Macros
- 350 Calories
- 12 g fat
- 32 g carbs
- 22 g protein

Makes a couple of servings.

Instructions:
1. In a large pot, heat the olive oil over medium heat.
2. Put the ground beef and cook until the color darkens a bit, go on stirring.
3. Put together the sweet potatoes, spinach, carrots, and water in the desired container.
4. When it reaches the temperature needed to boil, reduce the heat to low and settle for half an hour or until the sweet potatoes are ready.
5. Let it cool completely.
6. Then, serve it to your pet dog.

Comments:
....
....
....
....

Recipe 88	Turkey & Veggie Puree

A nutritious meal rich in protein can help dogs build a decent muscle mass.

Ingredients:

- 2 lb. lean ground turkey
- 1 bowl cauliflower florets
- 2 tbsp. raw turkey or chicken liver (finely diced or pureed)
- 1/2 zucchini (sliced)
- 2 medium carrots (coarsely minced)
- 2 tbsp. olive oil
- 1 bowl broccoli florets
- 1 ½ cup water

Macros
- 422 Calories
- 23 g fat
- 6.7 g carbs
- 47.3 g protein

4 servings

Instructions:

1. Add 1 ½ cups of water into a double boiler.
2. Put the carrots in a steam basket and then place it at the top of the pot then cover.
3. Bring to a boil and then reduce the heat to low until the carrots are soft.
4. While waiting for the carrots, you can start cooking the turkey and liver by putting them in a large skillet and heating them over medium-high heat. Do this until there are no more pinkish colors on

the meat.

5. Remove the liquid from the turkey and get rid of the fats from the drained liquid.

6. For 6-8 minutes, top it up with broccoli, cauliflower, and zucchini together with the carrots.

7. Once the vegetables are cooked, you can chop them to your desired size.

8. Now, add the minced vegetables to the turkey and liver, and mix them meticulously. Add the olive oil afterward.

9. Let it cool fully.

10.   Then, serve it to your pet dog.

Comments:

....

....

....

....

| Recipe 89 | **Meatballs Fiesta** |

What other treats can you give your dog but a good old classic meatball? Here's a meatball recipe that will make the man's best friend happy.

Ingredients:
- 10 lbs. ground beef (lean)
- 3 slices bread (cubed small)
- 2 cups oat bran
- 4 eggs
- 3 cans of pumpkin puree
- Salt to taste
- 4 carrots (boiled/ steamed and mashed)
- Flour
- Leaves of 4 kale stalk minced finely

Macros
- 492 Calories
- 15.6 g fat
- 12.3 g carbs
- 71.8 g protein

Makes 20 pieces.

Instructions:
1. Mix all the ingredients in a large bowl.
2. Make a ball shape with the mixture (can make 20 pieces).
3. Heat the oven to 400° F and bake the meatballs.
4. Cooking time depends on the size of the meatballs made (standard size usually takes 25 minutes).

Comments:
....
....
....

Recipe 90	Chili

You might be shocked to see chili for a dog, but it is not what you think it is. This is just a fancy name for a fancy treat you can make for your dog.

Ingredients:

- 4 carrots
- 1 can tomato paste
- 2 tbsps. butter
- Beef broth without salt
- 1 lb. ground beef
- 1 can corn (if preferred)
- 1 oz. macaroni

Macros

- 328 Calories
- 11 g fat
- 25.7 g carbs
- 32.1 g protein

5 servings

Instructions:

1. Heat macaroni in a pot while you cook the beef in a frying pan.
2. Put together the carrots, corn, tomato paste, and butter to the beef and cook for approximately 5 minutes.
3. Place the beef mixture into the pot of macaroni, add the beef broth, and mix well.
4. Place the mixture in an oven and cook at 350° F for about half an hour.
5. When its temperature lowers a bit, you can serve it to your dog.

Comments:

....

....

....

Recipe 91	Doggie Meatloaf

A soft and tender classic meatloaf with a mix of veggies for a healthier meal that your dog deserves.

Ingredients:

- 1 lb. lean ground beef
- 1 ½ cup grated mixed vegetables
- 2 eggs
- ½ cup cottage cheese
- 1 ½ cup rolled oats

Macros

- 278 Calories
- 8 g fat
- 19 g carbs
- 30.9 g protein

Makes 6 pieces of meatloaf.

Instructions:

1. Put your oven to 350° F.
2. Put together all the ingredients in a bowl.
3. Place the mixture evenly on a loaf pan.
4. Bake the mixture in the oven for 40 minutes.
5. After baking, place the loaf pan in the freezer.
6. Slice into meatloaf-size pieces.
7. Serve it to your pet dog.

Comments:

Recipe 92 — Spinach and Salmon Scramble

A seafood meal with a healthier twist by adding spinach.

Ingredients:

- 1 tsp. extra virgin olive oil
- 1/2 can salmon (3 ounces) (fileted and drained)
- 1/2 cup frozen minced spinach (thawed and drained)
- 2 eggs

Macros

- 287 Calories
- 19 g fat
- 1.2 g carbs
- 28.8 g protein

1 servings

Instructions:

1. In a non-stick pan, heat the extra virgin olive oil.
2. Add the salmon and spinach until evenly heated.
3. Time to place the eggs and mix until cooked.
4. Let it cool down.
5. Serve it to your pet dog.

Comments:

....

....

....

....

Recipe 93	Mini Omelets

These cute-sized omelets are a fancy treat for our cute dogs which they will be thankful for.

Ingredients:

- 3 organic eggs
- 3 green diced pepper
- 1 oz. smoked salmon (thinly sliced)
- Olive oil for greasing the ramekin

Macros
- 104 Calories
- 5.7 g fat
- 2.2 g carbs
- 11.1 g protein

Makes 3 ramekins.

Instructions:

1. Drizzle a small amount of olive oil on 3 ramekins, enough to grease the insides.
2. Crack the eggs directly on the ramekins then put the green pepper and the salmon.
3. Mix continuously with a fork.
4. Bake in the oven at 350° F for about 10-12 minutes or until the contents are cooked.
5. Let the temperature lower.
6. Then, serve it to your pet dog.

Comments:

....

....

....

....

Recipe 94 — Turkey and Pumpkin Combo

Here's another turkey recipe mixed with pumpkin. Another option is if pumpkin is the vegetable available for you.

Ingredients:
- 1 lb. ground turkey
- 1 bowl cooked pumpkin puree
- 1 bowl cooked brown rice
- 1 bowl minced zucchini
- 1 tbsp. coconut oil
- 2 cups water

Macros
- 315 Calories
- 10 g fat
- 31 g carbs
- 22 g protein

4 servings

Instructions:
1. In a large pot, heat the coconut oil over medium heat.
2. Place the ground turkey and cook until browned while you stir from time to time.
3. Add the cooked pumpkin puree, brown rice, zucchini, and water to the pot.
4. When you realized that it is already boiling, reduce the heat to low and simmer for 20-25 minutes or until the vegetables are tender.
5. Let it cool.
6. Serve it to your pet dog.

Comments:
....
....
....

CONCLUSION

This book on homemade dog food has aimed to provide pet owners with a comprehensive guide to understanding their furry friends and taking care of their nutritional needs. We have explored the different types of homemade dog food, including recipes that are easy to prepare, healthy, and nutritious.

We have also covered several aspects of pet dog care, including their habits, well-being, health issues, and interaction with the owner. It is essential to ensure that your dog receives the right nutrients to stay healthy and happy, and homemade dog food is a great way to achieve this.

As pet owners, we have a responsibility to ensure that our furry friends receive the best possible care, and this book is a valuable resource for anyone who wants to provide their dog with a balanced and healthy diet. By following the guidelines and recipes in this book, you can be confident that you are providing your pet with the best possible care.

In summary, this book has been a labor of love, and we hope that it has helped you to better understand your pet dog and provided you with the knowledge and tools to ensure that they live a healthy and happy life. Thank you for taking the time to read this book, and we wish you and your furry friend all the best!

References

10 Common Dog Health Problems | Poway Vet. (2021, July 28). https://www.animalemergencysd.com/site/blog/2021/07/28/common-dog-health-problems

A simple but effective feeding plan for adult dogs •. (n.d.). Honey's Real Dog Food. https://honeysrealdogfood.com/feeding-adult-dogs/

Bagga, M. (2022, April 11). Ways To Monitor Your Dog's Health At Home. DogExpress. https://dogexpress.in/ways-to-monitor-your-dogs-health-at-home/

Berg, S. H. (2023, January 19). 8 signs your dog is healthy. Nala Health. https://www.nalahealth.dog/za/8-signs-your-dog-is-healthy/

Blunt, W. (2021, May 28). The Benefits of Health Monitoring and Activity Tracking For Dogs with Betty Stearns and Scott Lyle (Episode 21). The Dog Book Company. https://thedogbookcompany.com/health-monitoring-and-activity-tracking-for-dogs-21/

Burke, A. (2021, September 21). Dog Allergies: Symptoms and Treatment. American Kennel Club. https://www.akc.org/expert-advice/health/dog-allergies-symptoms-treatment/

Burke, A. (2022, July 20). How to Choose the Best Dog Food. American Kennel Club. https://www.akc.org/expert-advice/nutrition/best-dog-food-choosing-whats-right-for-your-dog/

Cannon, A. (2020, August 24). Here's When to Take Your Dog to the Vet. Daily Paws. https://www.dailypaws.com/living-with-pets/veterinarian/take-dog-vet

D. Doctormmdev. (2017, July 13). When Should Your Pet Go On A Special Diet? Circle B Veterinary Hospital.
> https://circleb.vet/special-pet-diet/

How to Put Your Dog on a Diet. (n.d.). Small Door Veterinary.
> https://www.smalldoorvet.com/learning-center/wellness/dog-on-diet/

How To Tell If Your Dog Is A Healthy Weight. (n.d.).
> https://www.thepetexpress.co.uk/blog/dogs/how-to-tell-if-your-dog-is-at-a-healthy-weight/

Keeping Things Fresh: Pet Food Storage Guide. (2018, July 19). Fetch & Stay.
> https://fetchandstay.ca/blogs/news-blog/keeping-things-fresh-pet-food-storage-guide

Nutrition - General Feeding Guidelines for Dogs | VCA Animal Hospital. (n.d.). Vca.
> https://vcahospitals.com/know-your-pet/nutrition-general-feeding-guidelines-for-dogs

Randall, S. (2022, April 22). The Dog Supplements for Homemade Dog Food Meals You Need. Top Dog Tips.
> https://topdogtips.com/dog-supplements-for-homemade-dog-food/

TappyTaps.com. (n.d.). Barkio: Dog Monitor - 5 reasons why you should monitor your dog. Barkio.
> https://barkio.com/en/blog/article/5-reasons-why-you-should-monitor-your-dog

When Should I Take My Dog To The Vet? (n.d.).
> https://www.perrovets.com/blogs/when-should-i-take-my-dog-to-the-vet